Catholic Women in Ministry

Marie-Louise Ternier-Gommers

Catholic Women in Ministry
Changing the Way Things Are

NOVALIS

© 2007 Novalis, Saint Paul University, Ottawa, Canada

Cover design: Audrey Wells
Cover image: © W. P. Wittman
Layout: Pascale Turmel, Audrey Wells

Business Offices:
Novalis Publishing Inc.
10 Lower Spadina Avenue, Suite 400
Toronto, Ontario, Canada
M5V 2Z2

Novalis Publishing Inc.
4475 Frontenac Street
Montréal, Québec, Canada
H2H 2S2

Phone: 1-800-387-7164
Fax: 1-800-204-4140
E-mail: cservice@novalis-inc.com
www.novalis.ca

Library and Archives Canada Cataloguing in Publication

Ternier-Gommers, Marie-Louise
    Catholic women in ministry : changing the ways things
are / Marie-Louise Ternier-Gommers.

ISBN-13: 978-2-89507-839-5
ISBN-10: 2-89507-839-4

    1. Women in the Catholic Church. 2. Women clergy. I. Title.

BX1912.2.T47 2007   262'.142082   C2006-905350-2

Printed in Canada.

We acknowledge the financial support of the Government of Canada through the Book Publishing Industry Development Program (BPIDP) for our publishing activities.

5 4 3 2 1   10 09 08 07 06

NOVALIS

Contents

Acknowledgements

Thank you / Merci

To the 24+ women in northern and western Canada
who made such a generous offer of stories, experiences, insights
and perspectives.
Without you there would be no book.

To Ivan Buehler and Fr. James Gray, OSB,
for encouragement and a careful read of the manuscript "in utero."

To my editor, Kevin Burns, for his faith in me that I could write this
story, and for his careful mentoring through the literary challenges
this type of writing posed.

To Anne Louise Mahoney and all the staff at Novalis
– you do become more like family with every subsequent piece of
writing.

To my husband, Jim, for his unconditional love and faithfulness
through all the ups and downs of living with my ecclesial joys and
sorrows.

To Sarah, for her love and courage in making the journey.

Dedication

"Sarah, what are your dreams for the future? What do you want to be when you grow up?" I asked in the middle of our conversation. Sarah's eyes lit up as she blurted out, "I want to be a liturgist in the Church!" Her answer took me aback. How many 17-year-olds today dream of working in the Church with this kind of enthusiasm? At the same time I cringed. Slowly, I looked for words. "That's great, Sarah. But do you know that working in the Church is not a bed of roses for a woman?" Without missing a beat, she replied, looking me straight in the eye. "I already know that from the strife in our parish."

Several months after this conversation, I arrived at the parish one morning and was met by the parish council chairperson. His face spelled distress as he chose his words carefully. "At last night's meeting, parish council voted in favour of breaking your contract as our pastoral associate. I'm very sorry." He rushed to add that it was not my lack of professional competency, but more that "the parish is not ready for someone like you."

Still in shock over this abrupt ending, I met Sarah's mother on the street one day. She told me her daughter was devastated by my dismissal. She added that this only strengthened Sarah's resolve to want to make a difference in the Church so that this type of mistreatment could not happen anymore. I realized only then that Sarah had been watching me like a hawk. She had recognized in me a role model for her own journey. My conversation with Sarah became a bittersweet memory.

A couple of years went by. I took a job in another city. I heard through the grapevine that Sarah had graduated from high school and started university at a small campus in another province. One day, her mother phoned to inform me that her father, Sarah's grandpa, had passed away. After the exchange of condolences and memories of her deceased father, Sarah's mother added, "There's something else you need to know. Sarah has announced – not asked, but announced – that she will be preaching at Grandpa's prayer vigil. She feels called to do this."

My heart stopped. "I will be there," was all I could say. I went to church the evening of the vigil, knowing that I was about to witness something unique.

After the leader of prayer had proclaimed the Gospel, Sarah, now nineteen, slowly walked past Grandpa's coffin, and made her way to the pulpit / ambo. In the following ten minutes I witnessed the birth of a preacher-woman. Untrained as yet, yes, but Sarah shone with a determination, a heart, with clarity and compassion that have only one source: God. She spoke with unbridled love and passion. Her strong sense of calling legitimating her place in the pulpit, Sarah skillfully wove together her grandfather's life with the Word from Scripture and God's promise in Jesus. A tearful hush fell over the assembly. Her witness aimed straight into the hearts of the mourning congregation; there was nowhere to hide from its healing power.

I found Sarah after the service and locked her into a long embrace. Tears quietly ran down my face and hers. "Sarah," I managed to whisper, "your grandpa has just initiated you into an important part of your ministry in the Church. And what's more, he'll be there to support you all the way." Sarah sighed with both joy and sorrow as she rested her head on my shoulder, whispering back, "I know, I know."

To Sarah and her contemporaries
whose dreams set their hearts on fire
to live their vocation to ministry in our beloved Catholic Church.
May the sharing of our experiences
help them to learn from,
and be inspired by,
our example.
May our shoulders provide them
with a place to rest their heads
in times of struggle and fatigue,
and to stand on as they climb
the mountain of their own calling.

Introduction

In 1962, Pope John XXIII summoned the Second Vatican Council. Two thousand five hundred Catholic bishops from around the world, along with ecumenical representatives and about fifteen female observers, gathered in Rome for extensive meetings on all aspects of the Church. These meetings continued until 1965 and produced sixteen important documents. In order to understand the huge shifts that this Church Council brought about, we need to go back 400 years.

The turmoil of the Reformation, led by Martin Luther in the sixteenth century, had polarizing effects on the Church. The Council of Trent formulated its positions in a massive effort to defend itself against the "errors" of the reformers. Its hard-and-fast positions on liturgy, sacraments and theology gave us a Church that remained virtually unchanged for nearly four centuries. At the Second Vatican Council, the Church emerged from this deep-freeze. Finally freed from a defensive approach, the bishops and cardinals at Vatican II revisited the treasures, wisdom and practices of the early Church to lay the foundations for a comprehensive renewal within the Church today. It should come as no surprise that much of the resulting renewal turned out to address key contentions that the reformers had brought to the discussion table nearly four centuries earlier. Some of the reformers' "errors" turned out to be necessary corrections to the Church if it wished to continue to be the dynamic presence on earth of the Body of Christ. Given the human nature of the Church, and thus its vulnerability to sin and error, such a body, even in its divine and sacred origins in Christ, is nevertheless always *Ecclesia semper reformanda est*: the Church in need of reform.

Whether the sixteenth-century Reformation and the resulting splits in Christianity benefited women remains hotly disputed. On the one hand, Martin Luther himself declared gender equality in marriage and the right to divorce, promoted the education of girls, opposed the veneration of saints, and believed that closing convents released nuns from sexual repression and male clerical domination. On the other hand, the initial good intentions of the reformers did not deliver for most women. In practice, divorced women, unless they were of marriageable age, faced a bleak existence. Few Protestant girls' schools were established and very few parents sent their daughters to school. Discontinuing the veneration of saints (male and female) deprived women of significant role models. And closing convents eliminated for women an honourable life choice other than marriage and family, a choice that fostered education, community, independence and responsibility, and gave women a semi-clerical status. In the Roman Catholic Church, a vocation to religious life has continued to be highly valued and respected for both women and men right up to our day. In fact, Vatican II gave each religious order a new challenge: to reclaim the charism of its founder or foundress and of its prophetic role in the Church.

And Vatican II did much more. The Council deliberations and documents reveal a church that changed its self-understanding from a "perfect society" to the pilgrim people of God bringing about the kingdom of God. The liturgy, celebrated in Latin and unchanged for four centuries, became "unstuck" when it began to be celebrated in the language of the people. After an overemphasis on the sacramental and Eucharistic dimensions of liturgy – an emphasis that had served as a way to differentiate and distance the Church from its critics at the time of the Reformation – Vatican II advocated and implemented the restoration of the Word of God to its rightful place of prominence. Selections from Scripture proclaimed in the Sunday Eucharistic celebration were expanded. The three-year cycle of biblical readings emphasized the importance of good preaching. The liturgical renewal sparked the creation of new prayers, refreshing thinking on decor and architecture, and new musical repertoires. The baptismal dignity and calling of the laity were rediscovered and reclaimed. New theological and historical thinking contributed to an unprecedented openness and respect toward Christians of all traditions and towards people of all faiths.

The fact that these and other changes occurred at all was nothing short of monumental. Pope John XXIII's summons to "open the windows" of the Church and to read the "signs of the times" was realized, both for the outside world and within the Church itself. Even now, well over 40 years after the Council, we are still interpreting and applying its insights and teachings. Church historians remind us that it takes approximately 100 years for a church council to have its full effect on the Church; we have only just begun. We will be appropriating the gifts of the new orientation and perspectives of Vatican II for several generations to come.

One of the fruits of renewal for which the Council Fathers laid the groundwork is the growing diversity of ecclesial ministry. The term "ministry" as employed in this book uses the following definition: "Ministry is a public service grounded in the Gospel and performed on behalf of the Christian community for the promotion of the reign of God."[1] Alongside a decreasing number of celibate men in ordained ministry, there is a virtual explosion of non-ordained professional ministry exercised by married men and, most particularly, by women. Like Topsy, these ministries just "growed."[2] This development has occurred with lightning speed over the course of a mere four decades. The necessary analysis, policy development and theological reflection, whether in official church documents at the local, diocesan and global level or in the literature at large, still do not adequately reflect this new pastoral reality. Nor do they afford this "new wine" of ministry its appropriate place of dignity, blessing and meaning. Much work in these areas remains to be done.

This book seeks to apply some of the discoveries of Vatican II to the concrete experiences of a small segment of these new ministers: Catholic women working in a variety of pastoral positions throughout western and northern Canada. Their experiences, self-understandings and insights are placed in the context of some key teachings of Vatican II. Most notably among these are the baptismal dignity and calling of all the baptized, the Church as communion and as pilgrim people of God, the inherent goodness of all creation, the renewed appreciation for the sacrament of marriage, the importance of following one's conscience and standing with the poor and vulnerable, the need for ongoing adult catechesis, and a new emphasis on the importance of pastoral gifts and responsibilities in the Church's ministers. Each of these teachings will inform the reflection and stories in the chapters that follow.

Some 26 Catholic women have joined me in this book. They have made a generous offering of their stories and insights, their joys and sorrows, their hopes and dreams. We live and minister in British Columbia, Yukon, Alberta, Northwest Territories, Saskatchewan and Manitoba. We work in many fields that, not that long ago, were the domain of clergy: parish life direction and administration; campus ministry; hospital and prison chaplaincy; retreat work and parish missions; Native ministry; pastoral assistance in urban and rural parishes; lay formation; adult faith education; diocesan, youth and freelance ministry. We lead faith communities in worship and offer pastoral care. We comfort the mourning and listen to the broken-hearted. We feed the hungry with God's Word and offer guidance to the seeking. We call forth gifts in the people of God in order to witness in the world to the Good News in Jesus the Christ. We regard our witness of love poured out in ministry as God's gift to the Church; it is a gift received with joy by most, while still viewed with suspicion by some.

An analogy with women in another time comes to mind. During World War II, women were recruited in great numbers to fill jobs previously held by the men who had gone off to war. All of a sudden, women found themselves working in factories, in civil service, in professional fields and in defence industries. Once the war was over and the surviving men returned, many women retreated again into the private sphere of their homes. However, something in society had irrevocably changed. Women had discovered a new sense of worth. Besides earning money for what they did, they grew in self-worth and self-reliance, and in solidarity with one another.

In much the same way, many women today initially fill ministry roles due to a shortage of priests. Sheer pastoral need causes us to land in positions and spheres of ministry that previously belonged to the ordained. Thus we feel caught between two worlds, much like our sisters did during World War II. In the process of "filling in," we, like them, have discovered a new self-worth, a God who calls *us*, and a new vision for ministry in the future.

Understanding comes in hindsight, and that includes our understanding of God's action in the course of history, both personal and communal. Looking back helps to pull the threads of God's calling activity from the complex twists and turns life delivers. In retrospective, I discover both newness and tradition in women's roles in pastoral ministry.

For some of us, our love and desire to serve the Church in ministry began as an early, unspecified dream. At first we live out this dream in marriage and parenthood; then it resurfaces in a different form and leads us into church ministry later in life. When Catholic married men desire a more explicit form of church ministry, they might consider the permanent diaconate (if their diocese has reinstated this ordered ministry). Should Catholic married women want to serve the Church more explicitly, there is no automatic direction or place for them. Much depends on the opportunities available. Some women have come to pastoral ministry out of their renewed study and discernment of gifts within their religious orders. Still other women, often younger ones, are now enjoying a new and growing openness to pursue their heart's desire, so they enroll in theological studies at an earlier age.

Our experiences and emerging insights naturally raise new questions. Are women in ministry a "temporary solution," until there are once again enough celibate men in the priesthood? Are our gifts and callings valued for their own merit, or are they merely poor substitutes for the "real thing"? Is our commitment to pastoral ministry witnessing to a God who is calling us back to the model of the early Church, when a diversity of charisms was bestowed on a variety of people instead of being concentrated in one person? Are we "priests in waiting" until Rome changes its discipline? Or are we a brand new phenomenon of lay ecclesial minister, a vocation and call separate from ordained priesthood but somehow more focused on "*intra ecclesia*" (i.e. within the Church) than on the universal call of all baptized Catholics to bring Christ into the secular world? Such questions emerge from our ongoing witness, but the time for answers may still be far off.

Without settling for quick and simplistic answers, we can argue that, unlike the experience of women during and after World War II, the phenomenon of today's lay ecclesial ministry is not an invention of the contemporary Church to solve a personnel problem. A close examination of the Church's beginnings tells us that it is possible that using lay women and men in ministry is more than a stopgap measure. Besides the traditional ordained roles of bishop, priest and deacon, the growing diversity of ministries reflects something the Church has done from its very beginnings. The Christian community engages the Gospel with every time, place and culture in history. The dynamic relationship between Scripture, tradition and history necessitates that Christ's call to discipleship be adaptable to the particular needs and features of those who live in each time and place. Such diversity is faithful to the dynamic relationship between the Christian community, the historical and social conditioning of time and place, the sources of its faith tradition and its central figure, Jesus Christ the Risen One.

History itself attests to the creative ways in which the Church has faced such cultural crossroads and challenges, questions and tensions. We stand in a long tradition of taking the "signs of the times" and letting them shape the life of the faith community. The Church's commitment to inculturation includes the orientation to let the best of the culture in which she finds herself shape the expression of our faith. One important sign of the times in the 21st century is the increasing role of women in the public sphere, something that Pope John XXIII himself signalled in his 1963 encyclical *Pacem in Terris*:

> Women are gaining an increasing awareness of their natural dignity. Far from being content with a purely passive role or allowing themselves to be regarded as a kind of instrument, they are demanding both in domestic and in public life the rights and duties which belong to them as human persons.[3]

In allowing the Church's expression of faith to intersect with the best of the prevailing culture, lay ministers give flesh and blood to Paul's theology of the Body of Christ with its diverse gifts and charisms, as described eloquently in 1 Corinthians 12. In our own time, these new ministries and new ministers respond to a need and to a call. The gifts of all the baptized are needed both in and outside the Church. Ordained ministers, more than at any other time in recent history, serve as pastoral catalysts who invite, empower and order the gifts and contributions of lay people. In a modern culture that is suspicious of traditional authority, it is essential to respond to the cultural challenge by fostering mutuality and collaboration rather than hierarchy and institution – in particular, by including the gifts and insights of women as partners in church leadership on as many levels as possible.

Even though our ministries are grounded in the Gospel vision of Jesus – a discipleship of equals – many of us shy away from political lobbying for church reform. This is not always due to fear of losing jobs or credibility. Rather, this hesitation is borne out of a concern that our witness may be misinterpreted as a quest for earthly power and not viewed as a manifestation of the Holy Spirit. It is easy and understandable to let our impatience fuel anger and bitterness. It is easy to think that we have an inside track on what God is doing in our Church today.

We are acutely aware, however, that our primary call is to be faithful to the ministry entrusted to us. We are not called to insist on being right or to draw premature conclusions. While tending to the daily needs of the people of God in our parishes, schools, hospitals, prisons and families, we seek to infuse the Church with new energy and inspiration for the future while leaving the rest up to God. As a good friend reminded me recently, we live our lives forward and we will understand them backwards, long after all of us have gone home to God.

My encounters with the 26 Catholic women whose stories infuse the pages of this book – through personal meetings, e-mail and telephone – have been a tremendous opportunity for conversation and challenge, inspiration and reflection. I have discovered similarities, differences and new questions. I have found soulmates, colleagues and role models. Except for my own story, the women's stories and contributions are woven together into profiles that are actually a composite of two or more individuals. At the women's own request, identities and situations have been altered to respect their privacy and to create a freer relational space in which they can speak what lives in their minds, hearts and souls. While I honour it, their request also saddens me. It is a sober reminder that women still do not feel safe offering the Church the reality of their experiences and insights, both positive and negative, without anonymity.

All 26 women contributed because they strongly believe that what they are living is not an isolated or private matter. While these experiences are deeply personal, they reveal facets of our corporate life as the Body of Christ. In a spirit of frank dialogue and deep love for the Church, this book is offered to the pilgrim people of God in their journey toward God's reign of peace, love and justice, especially those who follow in our footsteps:

> No one puts new wine into old wineskins; otherwise, the wine will burst the skins, and the wine is lost, and so are the skins; but one puts new wine into fresh wineskins. (Mark 2:22)

1

We Just Growed!

It is not only through the sacraments and the ministries that the Holy Spirit makes the people holy, leads them and enriches them with virtues. Allotting his gifts "at will to each individual" (1 Cor 12:11) [the Spirit] distributes special graces among the faithful. By these gifts, [the Spirit] makes them fit and ready to undertake various tasks and offices for the renewal and building up of the church.

(Lumen Gentium, 12)

I cannot remember not wanting to be in church. Of course, I enjoyed a good teenage rebellion, and accused everybody in church of being hypocritical, but I did not intend to become a hypocrite myself. The word "lukewarm" did not appear in my vocabulary. I either loved or hated religion, faith, and the Church. Given the new openness in the post–Vatican II Dutch Catholic Church in which I grew up, I could even be relatively free with my criticisms. If the main obligation was to spend one hour a week with God on a Sunday morning (which my family dutifully did, dressed in our Sunday best) and live the rest of that week in a manner untouched by that one hour (which my parents, dutiful and hard-working as they were, did), then what was the point? I evolved from criticizing and distancing myself from organized religion to radical expressions of faith and solidarity as the only way to be a credible follower of Jesus. While "going to church" became less compelling, working in the soup kitchen and taking part in anti-war rallies became for me new hallmarks of "real" faith.

But, strangely enough, even in the most critical phase of my adolescence, I derived an odd satisfaction from participating in liturgical ministries, one that had little to do with being "useful" at Mass. I loved proclaiming the Scriptures – the fire that would run through my veins caused an adrenaline rush, the kind that now occurs in the pulpit when I preach. As a teenager I would not have understood the phrase that the Word of God is alive and active. Hindsight makes me wonder whether I already had a "live wire" with the Scriptures back then. Singing in the youth choir lifted my searching young spirit to new heights, not to mention introducing me to the great group of friends I found there. More than 30 years later, I am still in touch with some of these women and men. Together we prepared monthly youth Masses, events that tapped my wild imagination and fed a youthful, experimenting spirit. I served as a Eucharistic minister and, to my surprise, felt a profound and odd appreciation in my heart for the privilege of distributing the body of Christ to fellow parishioners. So despite my vocal criticism of the hypocrites in church, participating in ministries gave me a sense of purpose and belonging that I knew I needed. I just did not know why.

*** MEETING SHARON ***

Years later, when meeting Sharon, we reminisce about those times. Like a sweet fragrance, her calm and quiet demeanour fills the parish office where we talk. This fragrance increases as Sharon speaks of her faith journey with an unusual intensity and joy. Smiling, she adds her musings to mine. "I volunteered for everything I was allowed to do: singing, dusting off the family Bible, proclaiming, and later serving Mass and teaching catechism," she says. "A girlfriend and I even played at saying Mass in the forest – everybody thought that meant I was called to be a nun!"

Becoming a nun was something no one ever mentioned in seriousness to Sharon or to me. Looking back, I think we surely displayed budding qualifications for religious life, qualifications pointing to a "vocation" – that sustained and informed way of being in which one finds the greatest fulfillment and develops one's fullest potential. We loved church, we had a desire for God, and we tried to pray once in a while, especially when we got stuck in undesirable situations.

But my adult years, like Sharon's did for her, took me down a different path. For many years I didn't move much beyond being a faithful volunteer at the parish and diocesan level. Now both Sharon and I are approaching 50, married and mothers of three adult children.

I find myself in a diocesan ministry of adult faith formation and in an unusual preaching ministry in the broadest possible sense of that term. I preach in Protestant and Anglican pulpits at Sunday worship, I write Scripture commentaries and reflections, and I give retreats and workshops.

Sharon finds herself in the role of pastoral parish administrator of a suburban parish. Her previous professional experience in managing a small office now serves her well. Responsible for the overall pastoral needs of the parish, Sharon coordinates volunteers for the many ministries and projects, and oversees the administrative and financial aspects of running the parish. "I coordinate Sunday Liturgies of the Word (when no priest is available), weekday Morning or Evening Prayer, and at times I will preach at these occasions," she tells me. "I work closely with an assigned priest from a neighbouring parish who provides sacramental ministry: Eucharist, funerals, anointing, baptisms, etc."

Who would have ever thought all this possible when we were teenagers?

*

It took years for my current ministry to take shape, years filled with a lot of "leaving." My youthful zeal to serve God in adventuresome ways took me beyond many borders from an early age. I left my own family and neighbourhood at eighteen. I left my country permanently at 22, thus also leaving behind my Dutch native tongue. I left my European, urban upbringing in exchange for rustic prairie living in western Canada, far from dense populations and fast-paced living. I left modern conveniences when my prairie farmer husband and I opted for wood heat and did lots of canning and freezing of food we had grown ourselves. I left my own church and sphere of education when I walked into the Lutheran seminary for the first time at age 34.

It seemed that God was forever pushing me to be on the move. My young spirit had sought insatiably for authentic faith and for my life's mission – what did God want of me? After some Catholic youth rallies in my Dutch home province, my thirst for meaning and for God led me across the border. I discovered Taizé at age eighteen and Jean Vanier's l'Arche community at age nineteen. Since both were located in France, I crossed my country's border, never to live "back home" again. The world gathered at both Taizé and l'Arche. I formed friendships with young women and men in Germany, Austria, Italy, the US and Canada. Our common search for God, and for God's mission in our lives, forged a bond that transcended language and nationality. I knew then that every boundary in life was artificial, an insight that would re-emerge nearly 20 years later when I embarked on theological studies among Lutherans, Anglicans, Presbyterians, Mennonites and United Church folk. This insight proved to be trustworthy, and guided a deepening and broadening of my sense of call to follow Christ.

Talking with Sharon reconnects me to these threads of God's calling throughout my life. My hunger for a real, live faith, my sense of belonging in church, my spirit's gravitating toward ritual, liturgy and prayer, all are things with which Sharon readily identifies.

*** HEARING LENORA ***

Listening to Lenora, currently in her early 20s and newly married, brings back fond memories of the more dramatic turning points in my life. It was on one of my early visits to the Taizé community that I was struck by Jesus' gift of his life and of God's desire to lay hold of mine. I remember then and there making a promise to God to live my entire life in service of Christ Jesus and the Gospel.

Sitting in Lenora's office on the university campus, we speak frankly of God's fire that entered our lives at a young age. Lenora's dark eyes light up as our conversation progresses. Her engaging style of speaking betrays both her youthful enthusiasm and her Italian background. Sometimes she is so animated that her long, wavy, dark-brown hair swings back and forth as if blowing in a fierce wind. Lenora readily remembers the roots of her desire for ministry:

> I vividly remember at age six becoming painfully aware of why Jesus died on the cross. That had such an impact on me that I wanted to give my life in service to him ever since. I volunteered for everything in the church, and from a very young age I had a passion for theology. I pursued my studies while also working half-time in a parish. Now, after six years (!), I have finally completed my studies and I'm excited about my new work as a campus minister.

In this capacity Lenora helps coordinate (and sometimes helps lead) liturgies in chapel, plans programming and Rite of Christian Initiation of Adults (RCIA), works with Protestant campus ministers on regular ecumenical exchanges and worship. She is also available to students for individual counselling. This ministry is her response to God's will, and she fulfills its responsibilities with gratitude and zeal.

*

I used to have some pretty simplistic ideas of vocation and God's will for my life. I thought that discerning what God wanted was like running through a maze full of random twists and turns, with only one correct way that would find me this promised exit called heaven. And somehow I had the false notion that the more dramatic my life choices were, the closer I must be to figuring out where God wanted me. Little did I know that vocation was not about acrobatics. It took more years of living to discover that the term "vocation" captures that deep, sustained joyful way of being, giving expression to the best I can be in both the Church and the world.

But when young and curious about the world, I was over-confident yet anxious, courageous yet fearful, unconventional yet conforming. Life was a circus, full of acrobatics and dramatic events. Proficient in four languages, I travelled to France, where I became a frequent visitor to Taizé. Eventually I left my job, my possessions and my family in the Netherlands to live in Taizé for four months. I became part of the core group of young adults who assisted the Brothers in the welcoming and accompanying of the thousands of young people who pitched their tents there each week. Following that rich and intense summer, I made a one-year commitment to Jean Vanier's l'Arche community of people with disabilities in Trosly, France.

While my experience in Taizé had deepened my spirituality and my commitment to God in Jesus Christ, my year at l'Arche gave me an opportunity to give concrete expression to this commitment. I have shared some of those experiences in a previous book, *Finding the Treasure Within* (Novalis, 2002). Personal connections and friendships formed through l'Arche and Taizé eventually landed me in Canada. Meeting and marrying a mature and handsome bachelor prairie farmer sealed my fate.

The first dozen years of married life were filled with raising three children, hauling wood and drawing water, and growing and preserving our annual winter food supply. The shift from a childhood in the Netherlands – in a home above my parents' store without any garden, front or back – to the idyllic and remote setting of a farm on the shores of a picturesque lake in the Saskatchewan parklands at the end of the municipal road (the end of the world, in my mother's eyes) seemed pretty radical to me. This must be it – God's will; I had arrived.

Life on the farm indeed settled into a pleasant and fulfilling routine with hard but healthy and satisfying work, three thriving children and a loving husband. However, after years of being one of the faithful volunteers that kept a parish humming, the old restlessness resurfaced. What did God want from me? Where and how was I called to serve? Was there something more to explore, something more that beckoned me? I had heard the same restlessness echoed in Sharon's words, like an old divine melody in our soul that keeps luring us beyond ourselves to ever greater things. But this time, with three children under ten, a labour-intensive, time-consuming land-based lifestyle, and a home far from everywhere, much water had gone under the bridge for me.

My simplistic ideas about how to discern God's will were forced to undergo some refinement. This second round at seeking God's will

– this time taking me into academic studies and a professional career – brought its own frustrations. The old image of God as the big magician who makes something appear if only I press the right button was still lingering in the corners of my mind. Fortunately, it was forced to die. Instead, it seemed that God was speaking in cryptic messages that needed interpreting and decoding.

Sharon laughs when I tell her about this. "I know this feeling all too well. God pulls on my heart strings but I still need to figure out how to respond in concrete commitments," she says. For Sharon, this means listening to both internal and external signs in her life, and bringing these to prayer where they are scrutinized in the light of Scripture, meditation and reflection. This process includes in no small measure the concrete realities of life circumstances and opportunities.

*** MY CURRENT JOURNEY ***

Meeting women like Sharon and Lenora has become critical to my own understanding of God's call and my response in ministry. For practical reasons, I had chosen a Lutheran seminary; it was "only" a two-hour drive from the farm. The nearest Catholic theological school was a four-hour drive away and therefore out of the question for a woman with three children under ten, a woman married to a farmer who was also married to his land.

The Lutheran seminary community was most hospitable to non-Lutheran students. Attending this ecumenical place of formation and learning gave me lots of female peers and role models, but there were few female Catholic role models in rural Saskatchewan. Much of my current journey in ministry had occurred, therefore, in isolation.

Discerning a call to ministry is different for Catholic men than for Catholic women; men have more official options available to them and have access to priests, bishops or religious men to help them discern. Since women who do not choose religious life, and certainly married women, are not considered to have any kind of formal call to ministry in the Catholic Church, I had no access to a formal ecclesial process of discernment or testing of such a call.

Nevertheless, I kept in regular contact with my bishop. I understood intuitively that ministry needs the protection and mandate of the Church, and I did not consider myself an exception. Apart from respectful personal conversations with him, no concrete suggestions or invitations came from the bishop. How could I evaluate the authenticity of my ministry experience outside of my own mind and heart?

Motivated by this deep need to connect with others and to place my experience in an evaluating light, I went looking for, and found, women like Sharon and Lenora, and all the others who appear in this book. It is in that search that I found inspiring role models and supportive colleagues. It was a relief and affirmation to find that others had experienced a similar kind of isolation, albeit lived in ways different from mine. Our stories are unique yet universal, fascinating and in some ways timeless. Where did we come from and how did this development come about?

*** DARLENE'S DREAM ***

Darlene now works with Wylma in team ministry to First Nations people in both urban and reserve settings. I have known about their team ministry for many years, and it is a delight to sit down with both of them. With a wit only Darlene can muster, she recalls the early awakening of her calling.

> My vocation began at the early age of eight, with a religious experience in which I knew I was created by the Father, gifted by the Spirit to the Son for the sake of his people. It was very much a call to work within the Church as best as a young person could do. At age 12, I became the summer sacristan for the parish church with the "keys to the Kingdom." When "working" I locked the door, stood at the altar and read aloud from the lectionary. I preached to imaginary listeners. In other words, I practised for ministry, which is my current pastoral and catechetical involvement with Native people. Already at that age I experienced frustration with the limitations placed upon women in the Church, but I was determined to stretch the boundaries whenever possible.

Sipping my tea, I listen with great interest as Darlene continues.

In my 30s, I had another prayer experience that redefined my vocation. As I prayed one night during a 30-day retreat, I heard a voice in the room saying aloud in the words of Christopher Marlowe's poem, "Come live with Me and be My love."[4] From that time on the focus changed from doing to being.

Darlene's vocation in the Church remains very much an expression of her baptismal call as she perceived it at the age of eight: giving her life completely to God in the person of Jesus through service to others, especially the most marginalized. "In practice," she says, "this means serving others in First Nations communities, bringing hope and healing."

*

Connecting with Catholic women such as these across western Canada has broken my isolation. The recognitions in one another's stories forge quick and deep bonds of sisterhood and collegiality. As well, I now have a larger context in which to place my own experiences and insights. I have discovered that the stories of others echo pieces of my own. Moreover, the teachings of Vatican II have been providing each of us with unique and reliable support and guidance. The notion that the Church is the pilgrim people of God (of which we are members) invites us to take ownership of the life of the Church. Restoring the dignity of the baptized and affirming their calling in both the Church and the world to bring about God's reign makes us responsible to develop and use our God-given talents. Women in ministry are doing just that.

It is inconceivable that the Holy Spirit would leave the pilgrim people of God, the Body of Christ on earth, without pastors at this time of a growing shortage of priests. In many ways lay ecclesial ministers are new "pastors," embracing new, yet ancient, expressions of service. Yet all this means that I, and others, simply took seriously the call from Vatican II to all the baptized to claim our dignity as daughters and sons of God in Christ Jesus our Lord. New emphases on the Church as mystery, as the pilgrim people of God, and as a sacrament of Christ's presence on earth have created intellectual, emotional and spiritual spaces in which we can be affirmed and within which we now grow to a mature adult faith.

It should not come as a surprise that a mature faith awakens gifts. Adulthood in society compels us to make a meaningful contribution to the well-being of our world. Adulthood in faith increases our desire to share the Good News and to offer our talents at the service of that Good News. For some of us, this maturing in faith comes with a desire to share such gifts in pastoral ministry. When we grow in insight and understanding, when we grow in an intimate relationship with God through Jesus, the desire to share and proclaim that which gives such life to the full grows equally. When we tap the rich sacramental and liturgical life of the Church, we grow a natural desire to point others in the same direction, because we find such abundance there.

And so what I discerned among the Lutherans – the reawakening of a teenage dream to serve the Church in ministry – is in fact affirmed and celebrated by the theology and spirituality of Vatican II. When church teaching fails to reflect the human experience, the Church risks disconnecting itself from its members and loses the power to be a source of guidance and inspiration. My experience became the opposite: my personal experience not only matched the theology and spirituality of Vatican II, but also I recognized in the Vatican II documents that a call to lay ecclesial ministry is a valid call, and that it can bear all the features of God's calling activity.

*** MILLIE'S CALL ***

As soon as we meet, I like Millie, a woman in her late 50s. Her bubbly nature, combined with a strong maternal instinct, makes any stranger feel comfortable. Millie illustrates the radiant promise of new ministries:

> Wherever I have ministered, I have loved to be among the people and have been well-loved! One parish I went to, I stayed for ten years, and it was one of the most heart-wrenching experiences of my life when I decided to leave. However, I knew I was burned out and needed a change. Years later, I was told, by both clergy and laypeople, that I had been one of the best things that had happened in the parish. When there was a change of personnel several years later the new pastor called to ask me to return. This has been very affirming to me.

*

Millie and I share a deep joy. Being among the people, touching them in their everyday lives, seeing them through the joys and crises that life brings, are all privileges as well as sources of God's revelation for each of us. Acting as God's instrument to mediate people's encounters with God fills us with both fear and praise. One of Millie's own children died of cancer in her early 20s. Millie experienced intimately how the joys and sorrows of ordinary people are the holy ground where God enters our lives. "To have suffered at my daughter Karen's bedside and to grieve her passing was painful, but was also a deep experience of God's intimate involvement with us and of God's everlasting faithfulness," Millie recalls. Unbeknownst to her, this crucial piece of her own agony, her "Gethsemane," became a training ground for her current ministry. To be allowed into people's intimate spaces of life brings joy, affirmation and reverence to our task as pastoral ministers and serves as a confirmation of that calling. Fruits such as these confirm one's vocation.

Millie continues:

> After a time away from the parish, in high school ministry and in hospital ministry, I felt again the pull to return to parish ministry. I learned through one of our priests that the parishes where I am presently serving were without a priest. Three months later, I received a call from the chancellor, asking me to accept the position.

*

Studying the history of early Christianity taught me that the early church communities teemed with committed and mature disciples like Millie, Sharon and Lenora. Women and men served in a wide variety of ministries. The first few centuries saw a broad acknowledgment that the gifts of the Spirit were being showered abundantly on all the baptized for the building up of the Body of Christ, the Church. Opportunities abounded to share those gifts in practice. As St. Paul wrote to the Ephesians,

The gifts [Jesus] gave were that some would be apostles, some prophets, some evangelists, some pastors and teachers, to equip the saints for the work of ministry, for building up the body of Christ, until all of us come to the unity of the faith and of the knowledge of the Son of God, to maturity, to the measure of the full stature of Christ (Eph 4:11-13).

Not only was my isolation broken when I connected with other Catholic women in ministry; I also recognized a connection across time and place with the early church communities, where women and men served in a diversity of ministries. This realization was nothing short of feeling welcomed into a communion of saints that, as Elizabeth Johnson says so well in her book *Friends of God and Prophets*, embraces past, present and future:

> Our interpretation parses the communion of saints into five rudi-
> mentary elements: the community of living, ordinary persons as
> "all saints," in particular as this designation is used to characterize
> members of the Christian community and their relationship to the
> triune God; their working out of holiness through creative fidelity
> in ordinary time; their relation to the circle of companions who
> have run the race before, who are now embraced in the life of God
> and accessed through memory and hope; the paradigmatic figures
> among them; and the relationship of this community, living and
> dead, to the whole community of the natural world.[5]

In the first few centuries this fledgling band of disciples, this new "Way," grew in size and scope. Such expansion increased the need to organize and centralize church leadership for the sake of good order. And so it was that, over the course of several centuries, this centralization developed to the point that it became understood that a call to serve God's church now meant ordained ministry as bishop, priest or deacon – as of the twelfth century, ordination exclusively for celibate men – or religious life (for celibate women and celibate men). In particular, looking back into those early centuries offered me a new configuration of meaning. Maybe what I was experiencing as this burning desire to serve in pastoral ministry was not so strange after all.

Could it be that God's activity in my life, and in the lives of many
women and men today, was in fact continuous with what God has
always done: raising up a variety of women and men, setting them
on fire with the Gospel of Christ, and sending them out in ways that
curiously resemble what happened in the early days of the Church?
Today's explosion in lay ecclesial ministry resembles a former time, a
faint memory in the Church's heart and mind, much in the same way
as we ourselves now walk back through the twists and turns of our
own personal lives to ponder how we ended up in a place of pastoral
ministry at this time and in this place.

And so we arrive at today's phenomenon of pastoral ministry exercised by non-ordained women and men. This current practice has
several effects. Developing among those who remain in the Church
is a broadening and deepening of the faith life of the people of God,
the Body of Christ. Others argue that lay ecclesial ministers stretch
and challenge the Church in its traditional understanding of leadership models. The Spirit of God takes radical freedom in doing a new
thing, the argument goes, and we ought not to stifle and control that
Spirit.

A centuries-old clear and hierarchical model of leadership and gover-
nance now looks suspicious in a postmodern culture with its strong
distrust of traditional institutions. The development of lay ecclesial
ministry occurs against the backdrop of an overall drastic decline in
church attendance and in the number of ordained ministers. These
and other developments in both Church and world make this time
one of pruning, testing and transition for the Catholic Church. At the
same time, God's newness always appears in the embers of the old. In
the midst of a growing secularization of Western culture, the Church
is nevertheless being renewed and reshaped by the divine Potter.

Such times of profound change create a challenging context that
needs articulating and reflecting upon. While theological, ecclesio-
logical and social analyses are the domain of competent professionals,
I believe that, as women in ministry, we live and work in the liminal
space created by these times of change. Women exercising ecclesial
ministry in the 21st century do so in a secular culture that is no longer

driven by Christian values and by consensus, and in a Church that can no longer rest on traditional forms of authority and leadership.

*** DEANNA'S PASSION ***

Not every woman currently serving in pastoral ministry had fond childhood church memories and a strong desire to serve the Church. Deanna is the kind of person you don't forget easily once you've met her. Short in stature, she shoots from the hip. The spark in her eyes grows fierce with joy and pride as she tells me of her journey back into the Church, and then into ministry. Even though I connect with Deanna's passion for the Scriptures and for ministry, and with her intimate spiritual encounters with God, her beginnings are quite different from mine. But those very differences remind me that God can use everybody.

> I work in Catholic prison ministry. I know all about living the wrong values. As a young adult I turned my back on the Church, and I was convinced I could handle life without God and without religion. When my marriage broke up and I found myself with two children and no supports – no resources, no money, no job, no friends – there was nowhere to turn but to God.

I sense her memory of despair as she recalls those early years.

> Being skeptical, I walked into a church one afternoon and asked God to give me another chance – in turn I promised to give God another chance. I remember the glow that covered me so suddenly and completely that afternoon as I sat desperately alone in the pew. Yet I remained deeply distrustful of that sensation for a long time.

Deanna pauses, lost in thought. I remain silent, knowing there is more coming.

> Eventually I attended an evangelical church and – surprise! – I sensed the need for confession, something I had not done since Grade 4! In the course of that following year, a welcoming evangelical church and an understanding Catholic priest became my new mentors on a spiritual journey that was unknown territory for me.

> Over time, God used the twists and turns in my life to bring me back to the church of my youth. Once I grew a mature faith, gifts and callings to ministry were awakened along with a desire to offer these gifts to the Church in gratitude for the healing and belonging I found there.

She smiles with a fresh injection of that gratitude with which she exercises her ministry. We sit together, sharing this holy moment of recognition on one another's journey.

The twists and turns of Deanna's life culminated in a deep faith and rich ministry, but this development did not exactly come out of nowhere. She possessed gifts and abilities and a natural disposition to serve in ministry. All she needed to do was to nurture what was already present in her, and to configure her gifts and skills for the work of ministry.

*

The old dictum that "Grace builds on nature," as illustrated in Deanna, is confirmed in my own life. The gifts and abilities I displayed in marriage and family life, and in the workplace, were simply called forth in a different configuration for ministry. They were further deepened and refined through my studies, and subsequently led me more specifically into ministry in the wider Church. My values of integrity and faithfulness now became sources of strength, supporting my commitment to creative and faithful expressions of pastoral ministry, even if these forms have lain buried in church history for many centuries. Thus, in a world afraid of permanent commitments and suspicious of institutional authority, the witness of married Catholic women in pastoral ministry can be a countercultural sign.

*** GLADYS'S VOCATION ***

My surprise upon meeting Gladys unmasks my own stereotypes about religious sisters, because Gladys doesn't fit any of them – I should know better by now! Dressed in jeans and a T-shirt, with her greying hair in one long braid, she welcomes me with tea and bannock at the residence of her religious order in Edmonton, where she is spending some days off. Our conversation makes me realize that religious sisters find themselves in a similar place of countercultural witness in a world where most people are afraid of permanent commitments and distrust institutional authority. Gladys drives this point home when she explains,

> My vocation is to be a sister of the Institute of the Blessed Virgin Mary (IBVM), and my particular calling is to walk with aboriginal people in pastoral ministry. I am in my late 50s and walk in the footsteps of my British foundress Mary Ward, who lived from 1585 to 1645. After her example, I know that my intimate faith relationship with Jesus propels me to faithfully serve the Church in unconventional yet fruitful ways. My ministry consists of "being with" the people as a way of walking with Christ and his people.

Mary Ward founded a non-cloistered religious order for women patterned on the charism and ministry of the Jesuits. She experienced much resistance to this initiative, as it contravened the decrees of the Council of Trent (stating that all women religious are to be cloistered). Moreover, the Jesuits considered a female counterpart to their existence "ludicrous." Nevertheless, Mary Ward persevered in the face of the Church's own disapproval. In 1877, over two centuries after her death, the Institute of the Blessed Virgin Mary gained public recognition and was allowed to claim Mary as their foundress.

As a pastoral and spiritual leader in Canada's remote north, Gladys understands her task to be transforming the parish into a family and to walk with people: "The community's isolation makes people very reliant on one another in ways rarely found in populated areas in the south," she points out. Gladys has finally found her place in God's plan both as a religious sister and as the pastoral administrator for several parishes in a remote northern region of our country. She felt a call to religious life very early on in life, but ignored it. Like Jonah in the Old Testament, she tried to make the call go away by travelling and living overseas. But God continued to call her, gently yet persistently, into religious life and then more specifically into pastoral ministry. Vocation is like that – when the beckoning voice in our heart does not go away, when it persists in speaking to us through various circumstances and people in life, when the dream refuses to die despite the obstacles standing in the way of its realization, we do well to pay attention. The promise of abundant life is hidden in that inner and outer persistence.

*** FRANCINE'S CHOICE ***

In my search, I discovered some women who live their vocation and ministry not as wives or professed religious, but as single women in the world. To remain single can be a conscious life choice, even a sign of protest in our Western culture, which is overly occupied with sex. To choose the single life apart from a commitment to a religious community is not only a challenge in the world, but also in the Church. Francine is 44 and has never been married, nor has she ever been a "sister." She often faces puzzled looks from good Catholics when they discover that she is not attached to a husband or a religious community. She has had to clarify frequently that a call to ministry does not automatically entail a vocation to religious life.

> I am a woman who has been called by God to a life of celibacy and of service to the Church. The first priority is to be in relationship with God in and through Jesus Christ. God asked, "Will you?" and I said, "Yes."

Now involved in retreat work, Francine's career in the Church covers a wide range. She has been a parish music coordinator and catechist. She has held positions in diocesan ministries, most notably in liturgy, RCIA, youth ministry and adult faith formation. Her gifts in administration and organization, as well as in teaching, have served her well in these various roles. Her natural compassion, her regard and respect for people, her patience and joy make her a highly effective minister of the Gospel.

*

Even though we who are women ministers in the Church do not all belong to religious orders, our inspiration in ministry comes from pioneer women who charted new territory in both the Church and the world. Founders of religious communities, missionaries, teachers moving across the prairies – all had a sense of moving into the unknown.

Doing ministry in some type of professional capacity – ministry that requires a certain level of education or formation, is paid and has a formal mandate – truly feels like venturing into unknown territory. For years I was comfortable with the obvious volunteer jobs: cleaning the church, serving in liturgical ministries, helping with funeral lunches, coordinating volunteers, teaching catechetical classes, facilitating children's liturgy, and even serving as an occasional leader of prayer.

Then I received new invitations in pastoral ministry as an expression of a vocation. Those who lost loved ones began to call on me for pastoral care and for leading them in the liturgical farewell of the deceased. Protestant and Anglican congregations invited me to preach and break open the Word of God in their pulpits. Groups of all Christian backgrounds asked me to lead retreats and workshops. Publications offered opportunities to write Scripture commentaries and reflections. Each of these forms of ministry – in a pulpit, in a publication, in a funeral chapel or a retreat centre – has a public component of witness, leadership and modelling. Service is expressed, not in volunteer ministry, but in a formal leadership capacity. When women move from volunteer service to leadership ministry in the Church, commitment to integrity, accountability and prayer increases dramatically.

Women in pastoral ministry might be regarded as newcomers, but we have contributed to the life of the Church in the world for centuries. Many of the first pastoral ministers in the 1970s and 1980s were women religious. This is not surprising, considering that women religious have also been pioneers throughout the world in education, health care, social services and countless other forms of service to people in need. A recent US study showed that even as recently as 1990, 41 per cent of paid lay ministers were women religious; this percentage dropped to 16 per cent in 2005.[6] "For the first time [...], there are more paid professional lay ministers in our parishes than there are priests," said Father Eugene F. Lauer, director of the National Pastoral Life Center (NPLC) in New York, which conducted the study. In Canada as well as in the United States, increasing numbers of married and single women hear a similar call, and are joining, even replacing, sisters and priests in ministry inside the Church.

Throughout the ages, women have kept many a parish alive with their selfless generosity and quiet service. What is changing is that women are acquiring professional theological, liturgical and pastoral formation. We are slowly receiving appropriate ecclesiastical mandates and authority, even within the current restrictions, and earning salaries, however meagre. In this way we are becoming part of the public ministry of the Church and receiving increasing recognition for our contributions.

*** SHARON'S EXPERIENCE ***

The storehouse of gifts and abilities for ministry often comes from a life rich with previous professional, educational and personal experiences. Sharon illustrates this when she says,

> As a young woman teaching in Catholic schools and offering adult religious education sessions in the evening, I felt more and more the pull to leave the classroom and work with our adult population as well as with families, to bring about the reign of God. My first parish experience took place when I was sent by our diocese to a small city parish where the new pastor was recovering from a heart attack. I stayed there for about three years and I loved the variety of the work. I had many opportunities to touch people's lives at critical moments, as well as through adult education and preaching. The pastor appreciated my presence, and would happily say in jest, "You are the pastor! I am the assistant," and in all practicality, so it was.

I am clearly not alone in discovering that my career – what I do to earn a living – and vocation (that which taps my deepest joy and passion) have merged into one. The synchronicity between who we are and what we do creates a stark contrast to the fragmentation of modern living. The ensuing harmony between being and doing, between service and leadership, springing from the core of our heart, constitutes perhaps the most powerful confirmation of ministry. These are exhilarating moments. More than once I have felt such synchronicity as a way of being totally overtaken by Christ, as Annette explains below.

*** ANNETTE'S RESPONSE ***

We communicate only by phone and e-mail, but I sense an immediate connection with Annette's careful and clear manner of speaking. She tells me that, after 20 years of marriage, her husband recently died of cancer. She is still grieving this tremendous loss. Her only child is now in her last year of high school. Annette is eager to share her ministry experiences. I take notes as I listen with great interest.

In her capacity as pastoral associate, Annette prepares children and adults for sacraments. She provides one-on-one spiritual counselling and leads prayer services in schools, and for funerals, wakes and other occasions.

> Presence itself has become a central part of my "doing." I allow Christ to be present to the people through my eyes, my words, my tears even. In a way I consider this as acting *in persona Christi*, the phrase used to define the role of the ordained presider at Eucharist. The serenity with which I can now speak these words is the fruit of a long journey back to the Church. It is God's quiet and loving persistence in my heart that beckoned me, despite the pain and rejection suffered at the hands of that same Church.

I am all ears, but Annette does not want to elaborate, focusing instead on the gift of the here and now in ministry. I respect her discretion and listen some more.

> Looking back, I now recognize God's own guiding of my life to this current place of ministry. God used an army of people to pull me out of the pain, and I've come to call God the "Hound of Heaven" who won't give up on anyone.[7]

I remember the nebulous feeling that being led to an unknown place can cause. As I responded to God's call, I felt like a child whose mere curiosity takes her around the bend of a road she has never travelled, and who doesn't know how to get back home. I was terrified. I felt like Peter; someone else placed a belt around my waist and took me where I'd rather not go. The unknown bend in the road was my entrance into theology studies and pastoral formation. I began with what I thought was a clear plan: I would specialize in pastoral counselling in order to work in a counselling agency. I had worked for many years as a counsellor in a shelter for abused women and children; and

I had served on the board of Catholic Family Services. And so pastoral counselling seemed like a logical choice of studies. My keen interest in and compassion for people in crisis blended with my desire to bring spirituality into the caregiving and counselling I wanted to provide.

But as I devoured all learning not only in pastoral care and counselling, but also in theology, liturgy, preaching, Scripture and church history, the plan began to change without my conscious awareness. Was God's plan different from mine? Whatever brought on the change, in the plan and in my heart, I only discovered the change when it was too late to turn back. I have often imagined that God must have been laughing as I innocently dove into one course after another. The learning opened new vistas never noticed before. My spirit feasted on the rich new food. My dream expanded and my heart harkened to new songs.

Never before had I wanted something other than what God wanted; this time, for some strange reason, was an exception. I argued with God, stating that I'd be quite happy being "just" a pastoral counsellor. But arguing with what has come alive in the deepest core of one's being is futile, even though that did not stop me from trying. However hard I tried, though, the genie would not go back into the bottle. It was all rather ironic; for once I wanted something more modest than what God intended, or so I thought. Did I fear being thrown out of my comfort zone in the Church? Did I want to avoid rocking the Church's boat on the question of women in ministry? Perhaps. I attribute my current activity in several different fields of ministry clearly to God, because I could never have planned or expected most of them by myself.

Even though some of my ministry borders on freelance work, such as preaching in various denominations, I strive to remain firmly connected to the faith community. It is this direct orientation toward the community that makes ministry constitutively different from, say, operating one's own business. An inherent characteristic of ministry is that it needs the authority of the faith community to be exercised properly. I cannot very well hang up a shingle outside my door that says, "Have sermon, will travel." I need to be invited into the pulpit.

I have neither the power nor the right to put myself there without the community's permission.

*

As the face of pastoral ministry changes, so does the Church's self-understanding. The Second Vatican Council revealed a Church capable of rethinking its own identity and mission. After what looked like a 400-year freeze in time, theological positions, liturgical practices and cherished traditions were re-examined. These were held up to the Word from Scripture and were evaluated in the winds of change of contemporary society. The new formulations, comprised in the sixteen Council documents, are meant to equip all the faithful (laity, pope, priests and bishops) for the new challenges ahead.

The current development in lay ecclesial ministry illustrates such a new self-understanding. *Lumen Gentium* [Dogmatic Constitution on the Church] calls the Church a "mystery" instead of a timeless and static institution. Rather than a perfect society, the Church is a pilgrim people on the journey in solidarity with all of humanity toward God's reign of peace, justice and love. This Church is endowed with a dynamism in which the Spirit is forever doing a new thing: "By the power of the Gospel (the Spirit) rejuvenates the church, constantly renewing it and leading it to perfect union with its spouse" (*LG*, 4). When the time is right, and the Holy Spirit breaks through, great changes can indeed occur, even in the Church.

No one in the 1960s could have foreseen how extensively and profoundly the world would change in a mere 40 years, or how profoundly the world would remain the same. After two world wars, we may have thought humanity was on its way to global reconstruction and improvement, in particular with the vast developments in technology and the economic growth of most of the Western world. Prosperity was near at hand for the developing world, and goodwill was everywhere. Or so we thought.

Earlier periods in history have had their own share of turmoil: plagues, bloody wars and conquests, and missionary colonialism. Our time is no exception: terrorism, genocide, natural disasters,

HIV / AIDS, wars, mass starvation and exploitation of the poor are commonplace. In the modern Western world, consumerism, materialism and individualism have become new gods replacing the common good, faith in God, and institutional religion. It seems that we own more and we fear more: for our destiny, our planet, our resources, our relationships.

We may well be the first generation to experience the fact that the planet, creation itself, has limits, and to understand that we cross those limits at our own peril. Life may not continue much longer if we keep consuming of the earth's resources at the current rate. Short-term thinking driven by economics and self-interest by governments and big business puts us all at risk.

*** SOMETHING NEW ***

In the midst of this dismal picture, something new is being born. Nature, as well as history, shows that all pruning, transition and decay are already imbued with new life germinating in the midst of the chaos of change: "See, the former things have come to pass, and new things I now declare; before they spring forth, I tell you of them" (Isaiah 42:9). A fire kindled in one human heart does indeed have the power to set ablaze a new vision in the ashes of the old.

While ancient walls of what is past now crumble before our eyes, the Holy Spirit is busy rejuvenating the Church. We have only just begun this great adventure. God will not leave us without the means to declare the Good News of Jesus to a desperate world. Even though we cannot see the full picture, divine fingerprints are everywhere in this little piece of global renewal called Catholic women in ministry:

- the fire in the hearts of women desiring to serve in ministry,

- the overall affirming responses from local faith communities to the gifts women bring to ministry,

- the incredible odds many of us have had to overcome to respond to God's call, and

- the surprising opportunities for ministry opening up out of sheer pastoral need.

After I led and preached a four-day parish retreat with a colleague, one male parishioner confessed, "I admit that I wasn't keen on coming when I learned that it would be led by two ladies. But your witness changed my mind and heart. This is different, yes, but oh so powerful!"

When I doubt and question the authenticity of my pastoral work, God simply turns my face and invites me to look back over the points of divine encounter that have brought me here, as if to say, "Place your trust in me, and let me do the rest."

2

To Equip the Saints

The laity can be called in different ways to more immediate coopera-
tion in the apostolate of the hierarchy, like those men and women who
helped the apostle Paul in the Gospel, working hard in the Lord. They
may, moreover, be appointed by the hierarchy to certain ecclesiastical
offices which have a spiritual aim.

(Lumen Gentium, 33)

*** SHARON'S "SECRET" ***

A phone call disturbs our conversation this quiet morning. Could she
please come to the hospital soon? A parishioner has taken a turn for
the worse. Sharon replies in a reassuring voice that she will be there
within an hour. I notice her calm and caring way. I recognize that
she taps a source deep within her – I've done it myself. I ask what
grounds her ministry. "Baptism calls me to a way of being, identified
as one of service to God's community as leader, organizer, comforter,
listener," she replies.

At Vatican II, the Church recovered a theological understanding of
baptism that gives lay ecclesial ministers like Sharon and me words
and concepts to help name our ministerial identity, and to name
from whom these ministries take their lead. The Church teaches that
in baptism we are anointed into the priestly, prophetic and kingly
mission of Christ. For Sharon, her priestly role includes a mediating,
intercessory and sacrificial function:

I communicate and mediate God's love in the quality of my presence with parishioners. I bring the community's joys and sorrows to God in personal and communal prayer (intercessory), and I put aside my own agenda, my own pet peeves and hurts, in order to be fully available to the parish (sacrificial).

This notion of being anointed into Christ's own mission as priest, prophet and king fosters a spirituality of surrender, humility and sacrifice, a spirituality that, paradoxically, gives life to the full.

*

I remember a phone call just like the one Sharon received that morning. A woman phoned me in distress: her sister, elderly and single, had died. She told me that neither she nor her sister had much of a church connection. But then she said, "I heard you preach somewhere and I was moved by your words. So would you please consider doing my sister's funeral?" At first I did not know what to say. I encouraged her to contact a local pastor, but she declined. She wanted me. I took a deep breath, and tapped a source deep inside me – my anointing into Christ. In a calm and caring way I offered to meet with her and her husband. In the meantime, I did some investigating. I discovered that her sister's name was on the membership list at a local United Church. I spoke to the minister – a friend of mine – and explained the situation, saying that I was unsure of how to respond to the request about doing the funeral. "Look," he said, "obviously the connection with church is too remote for the family. They're not comfortable coming here. But she called you; something in her was moved by you and she's acting out of that. You, and I, need to trust this as God working in her life. All you need to do is to say yes. I will supply you with funeral resources and help you in whatever way you need." In collaboration with the funeral home and the United Church minister, I answered the call. I made the pastoral visit, gleaning the joys and sorrows of the life of the deceased through the eyes and words of the relatives who had loved her. I listened for God. I chose the Scriptures and wove the promises of resurrection in Christ into the woman's life and death in a way that respected the family's limited comfort level with things religious. I communicated with the funeral home and planned the liturgy. I led the assembly in the final farewell of their beloved sister and aunt. As Sharon demonstrated on that quiet morning not long ago, when the community calls us to be its minister, there is one answer: Here I am, Lord, send me as your servant.

*** OLD ENOUGH TO REMEMBER ***

Sharon is old enough to remember another time, a time when the laity were considered more like underlings than full members of Christ's Church who have worthwhile gifts and a mission that has both dignity and meaning for the Church at large. Even though Vatican II did away with such a dismissive view, Sharon reminds me that residues of this attitude still linger in both clergy and lay people today. Some parishioners view her leadership with suspicion. She feels more pressure to earn the people's respect than an ordained minister does.

> This is why my own spirituality and prayer discipline, as well as regular conversations with a spiritual director/confessor/mentor, are so important. These things help me grow inner resources that equip me to face the pressures and suspicions along with all the pastoral demands on my time, energy and attention.

I nod in agreement, thinking with affection and gratitude of my own spiritual mentors past and present.

Setting aside her own agenda, pet peeves and hurts does not mean that Sharon deems her own issues unimportant. On the contrary, she clarifies that developing vigilance and being committed to growing in self-knowledge and self-acceptance makes it possible to attend to her personal issues while not allowing these to hinder the quality of her pastoral ministry.

*

Ministry is an intimate form of relating to people. It requires that I engage with people in a generous, merciful and loving way, regardless of their political and theological views. Even if I cherish strong views that run contrary to those I serve, I need to park these lest they obstruct how I attend to the needs of this person, at this time, and in this place. Like the woman who phoned me with the request to do her sister's funeral, I must be free in heart and mind to listen for God, and to listen for the human plea. Sometimes, merely sharing a person's distress is more healing to the soul than providing quick answers or solutions. It is also more difficult, especially given my eagerness to fix another's pain.

I remember well the strife among music ministers in one parish. The pastoral challenge consisted of inviting a softening of hearts, a merciful spirit and an honest conversation. As the pastoral minister in the parish, I felt acutely the responsibility of this delicate task. At stake were the integrity of my own spirituality and my ability to be a pastoral leader to all parties involved. In preparation for the joint meeting, I spent time in prayer before the Blessed Sacrament. I offered to Jesus not only the conflict and the people affected, but also my own inadequacy and my own hardness of heart. I knew I could not invite others into a conversion of heart without first opening my own heart.

*** POWER OF BAPTISM ***

Sharon firmly believes in the loving power of baptism to open hardened and hurting hearts. She points to a photograph above her desk, showing a tall, smiling teenager at the baptismal font surrounded by the parish priest and some parishioners. "This young man gives me hope," says Sharon. She tells how Tyson started coming to church with his younger siblings. His mother is an alcoholic, and Tyson does not know his dad. Slowly Tyson discovered a family of friends in the parish.

"When something is happening at church, Tyson shows up," she says. "Often he brings his little sisters and brothers, his cousins and neighbours." Expressing initial signs of faith and a desire for greater belonging, Tyson enrolled in baptismal preparation with the parish's Rite for Christian Initiation of Children (RCIC) team. His mother promised to come on the Sunday of her son's baptism. Sharon vividly recalls how, throughout the service, Tyson kept one eye on the door, hoping against hope that his mother would come ... but she did not. And that hurt.

With a look in her eyes that tells me she was back at that memorable moment, Sharon continues.

> Tyson bowed his head over the font and listened to the voice of love that washed over his broken heart as the priest poured the water. In his young heart, he truly heard God's voice of love in a way that real life had deprived him of. For the first time, Tyson encountered a love so comprehensive that it would never let him down, and his heart was filled to the brim.

What is more, Sharon concludes, Tyson's very desire to belong challenged parishioners to take seriously their baptismal mission to be a true family in Christ.

To Sharon, examples such as this one reveal the power of baptism, a power that draws into divine Love those who know so little love in their lives and who feel adrift in a world without permanence, predictability and reassurance. At the same time, the Tysons in the world affirm for Sharon Christ's command to shepherd God's people.

> In John's Gospel Jesus asks Peter: "Do you love me?" When Peter replies, "Yes," Jesus says, "Feed my sheep" (John 21:17).

> Tyson makes clear to me that none of this ministry is for ourselves, nor does it originate with us. I have come alive to a deep sense of my identity in Jesus through baptism to bring the Good News of God's reign in a broken world full of Tysons.

Asking to be excused, Sharon heads for the hospital.

*

When our ministry bears these kinds of fruits, it is not hard to be in awe over the power of God to use the broken vessels of our lives as instruments of grace. And it is important not to take for granted that I am called to serve as God's vehicle of grace. Parish ministry has come with challenges and high demands, yes, but it also comes with an unusual and almost childlike trust that parishioners bestow on me in my role as pastoral minister. I am allowed into people's lives in ways that are neither accessible nor acceptable in any other role.

One day a man phoned, needing desperately to talk to someone. I heard the urgency in his voice, so I decided to put aside my plans for the morning. He came over, and we talked for more than an hour about the stresses in his relationships with significant others, but most of all about his struggle and desire to grow closer to God. Slowly the man's fretting and nervous tone of voice made way for a new peace and hope, communicated in a more relaxed posture and a calmer voice. It was an awesome experience to witness close-up how God's grace had once again touched one of God's children. My own understanding of baptismal calling grew and deepened through the encounter.

*** MARLENE'S MISSION ***

Marlene understands her call to ministry as arising clearly from baptism, and, in particular, the baptismal anointing into Christ's prophetic mission.

> My work brings me in contact with ordinary folk, fathers and mothers raising children, individuals struggling in the workplace or suffering breakdowns in relationships, seekers who long for an experience of God. But the pastoral nature of my work also makes me rub shoulders with others in pastoral leadership.

As a married woman called to a broad array of adult education ministries in several dioceses, and functioning in a church primarily accustomed to male, celibate, ordained leaders, Marlene feels acutely the prophetic nature of her pastoral mission. When she leads prayer, gives workshops or retreats, teaches or provides individual spiritual guidance, she knows that the recipients of her ministry are broken open into a new experience simply because a married woman occupies a place where they are used to seeing an ordained, celibate man.

> Sometimes being prophetic means that a "hard" word needs to be shared either through simple witness or through verbal statements. It means that I am called to bear witness to the truth by which I live in Jesus. I need to embody truth in conformity with the Gospel, in a spirit of humility and patience.

I need to refrain from seeking open conflict for the wrong reasons, and foster a certain "detachment" from being either right or wrong.

*

I share Marlene's greatest joy, which is seeing ordinary women and men awaken to the powerful depth of God's love for them, and to their own mission in the world.

*** PROPHETIC NATURE OF FAITH ***

Marlene sees her ministry as fostering what *Lumen Gentium* calls helping the laity to develop an appreciation of the prophetic nature of their faith "so that the power of the Gospel may shine out in daily family and social life" (#35). Marlene senses that a special power of conversion is activated through her ministry simply by the fact that she is a married woman ministering to married women and men.

> It's like they know I'm "one of them." With me an identification is possible, something which is more difficult when the speaker is an ordained celibate man. People can remain distant or theoretic, and be tempted to dismiss or minimize his challenges, because in their mind "he doesn't understand our reality."

*

I recognize this "mirroring" dimension of ministry. When I step into a pulpit, especially a Roman Catholic one, my hearers are already attuned to something new, simply because of a female presence in a place traditionally occupied by a male. Preaching done by "one of us" opens different hearing channels and employs different filters of understanding and interpretation. Such a unique identification is becoming more and more important in a culture so suspicious of external sources of authority and traditional institutions, a culture that has crept into our pews, sanctuaries and parish meetings.

Having a peer as one's model makes it much more difficult to keep an emotional distance from the witness and her message. Consequently, the recipient has fewer defences and is more open to let the message touch her heart. Listening and watching "one of your own" in a new ministerial role can awaken others to their own dignity and potential in non-verbal ways and at an unconscious level of awareness, a level that is much deeper than words alone can reach.

One woman in ministry automatically bestows respect and dignity on all women. A woman in a role of leadership and authority can access another's heart in ways different from a man occupying a similar role. Given the diversity of the people of God, it is clear that we need both male and female leaders in pastoral ministry to do the work of bringing about God's reign.

Slowly, a "chain of command" emerges: when it comes to claiming a call to ministry, God's call stirs the human heart and is confirmed ritually in baptism. Being called to ministry is consequently recognized, and invited to be exercised, by the community of faith. Inherent in each of these elements is a fourth one: a call into ministry needs to be authenticated by testing or purifying in a type of refiner's fire.

*** AUDREY'S TEST ***

Audrey, now a hospital chaplain, recalls, with a residue of pain,

> As a young child, I was an altar server. I played priest and could say the whole Mass. But then I became pregnant at a young age without being married. That cancelled any plans of entering religious life, which I thought was my vocation. While I finished my education and raised my child, I continued to attend Mass. I was so drawn to the liturgy, the sacraments, praying to the saints. But attending Mass as a young single mom was hard. Several parishioners shunned me in those days and wanted me to leave. I have forgiven them now.

*** SHARON'S PUT-DOWNS ***

Sharon, too, has known her share of put-downs.

> As a mother and wife, I volunteered in the parish, and prepared children for the sacraments. But different priests have been a real test. I've been told that I'm not knowledgeable enough to teach catechism, that I don't know my place in the Church, and that studying theology is not for women.

Once her children left home, a priest of a very different character and perspective came to her parish. He recognized her gifts and her desire, which had lain dormant for decades. He did not feel threatened by her but, to her great surprise, challenged her to use her gifts.

> Through his affirmation and steady guidance, my desire to learn, to study and grow in my faith was reawakened. When I landed in my first place of pastoral ministry, he continued to be there supporting and guiding me, praying for and with me. I have seldom met a priest who was so able and willing to listen to my ideas and who never put me down.

Sharon recalls the early days of her ministry "career." She found her call tested regularly by the parishioners themselves. That can be very rough at times! The biggest commotion ensued when Sharon changed from being a parish volunteer to becoming a member of the paid pastoral staff. The question of why she should get paid made the rounds at coffee hour. Her pastor was the most supportive person. He wanted the help of a pastoral associate, and responded to questions from parishioners. Sharon adds, "The paradox is that the people agreed Father needed extra pastoral help – they just didn't want to pay for it!"

*

My own testing has primarily come not from the people, but from ordained presbyters. Several times the faith community itself has called on me for some kind of teaching, guidance or other ministry. As I deeply respect good order and proper procedure, I would approach the parish priest with the community's request before proceeding with my response, clearly stating my preference to collaborate with the priest wherever possible and appropriate.

Such was the case when people from several different parishes approached me with the request for some basic training in preparing homiletic reflections. In Sunday Celebrations of the Word, especially in surrounding rural parishes, lay people often offered such reflections on the day's Scripture readings. Unfortunately, my invitation to collaborate with clergy on providing this type of training was refused, and was even regarded by some presbyters as a "meddling in priestly affairs." As a result, no training in lay preaching was ever offered. This type of refusal to work collaboratively frequently resulted in limiting my authority and my freedom to respond to the faith community. Many a time this threw me into a tailspin of doubt about my calling.

*** GLADYS'S CIRCUITOUS ROUTE ***

Gladys adds her contribution to our experience of these testing grounds.

> As I look back over my years of involvement in the Church, I can, in retrospect, see God's hand at work. What someone without faith would call coincidences, I call God guiding and leading me. Some of the steps on my journey have been very painful. It is precisely these, however, that have most affirmed my call. I took a very circuitous route to religious life and ministry in the Church, but I have grown into a more compassionate person because of it.

Gladys felt the call to religious life very early on but had no desire to answer. She was pretty sure God had the wrong number. Over and over, for more than 20 years, however, the call kept coming back, stronger and stronger until she could no longer ignore it.

> I had spent the bulk of my youth travelling and living overseas, always searching for the next big adventure. Yet when I decided I could no longer ignore God's calling, for the first time in my life I had a sense of peace and settlement that has stayed with me ever since. This has been a real affirmation for me that I have chosen the right path.

One of the biggest struggles for Gladys has been to find a religious order in which she could "fit." This was not an easy task for someone who had lived so independently all her life. It took persistence and perseverance to find a community Gladys can now call home. Gladys suffered additional testing in trying to explain her reasons to family and friends to live in the north and work for the Church, for virtually no pay. They could not seem to understand why Gladys would choose this with the education she had and the money she could make in the secular world.

Twice since moving here, I have been offered very good, very well-paying jobs that would involve moving away from the north and from this parish. I have not been the least bit tempted to accept. That was a real test for me. I feel that this is where I am called to be at this time and I am content with that. I know that I have made the right choice.

*** CARLA'S TEST ***

Carla, single and in her mid-30s, is employed in parish pastoral ministry. She pondered long and hard on the question of having her call tested. It seems to her as if the testing has never ended. It is nevertheless balanced by experiences of affirmation. In our interview she insists on reflecting on both testing and affirming at the same time.

For her, the most frequent form of testing comes from being a woman, and from not being ordained. The injustice of this response has drained Carla's enthusiasm many times. For the first five years of her ministry, she would simply work harder to prove herself, until her education, formation and pastoral standards exceeded the standards of priests.

Carla's competence and giftedness, however, made no difference when she was not given the opportunity to prove herself. It didn't matter how well she could preach, how effective she was at drawing the community together, what her pastoral gifts were.

> I was not regarded in the same category of usefulness simply because I am a woman. Sometimes this prevented me from being able to help people who needed pastoral care. If people do not give you the authority to help them, there is only so much you can do.

After five years of "proving herself," Carla felt discouraged and unsupported. To discern whether she was still called to ministry, she went on a 40-day Ignatian retreat. Such a retreat, in complete silence except for daily spiritual direction, is based on the Spiritual Exercises designed by St. Ignatius of Loyola, the founder of the Society of Jesus (Jesuits). Ignatius believed in the importance of engaging in prayer not only feelings, but also the intellect, memory, will and imagination to help retreatants discover God's will and purpose for them.

This retreat renewed Carla's personal relationship with Christ, and she has drawn a great deal of strength from the experience. She also learned valuable methods for continuously discerning her calling. "The spiritual freedom I found in this experience has empowered the past four years of my ministry," she admits.

*

Carla's experiences resonate with mine. When people reject my pastoral ministry or my role, I learn to meet them where they are. I pray, and trust the Holy Spirit to open their hearts. Often it has been a matter of time and letting people get to know me. Once they experience someone who is patient and accepting, they eventually allow me to serve them.

Over the years, Carla was encouraged to discover that the people who initially had the hardest time accepting her ministry often expressed the most appreciation for it later. But for others – parish visitors who left the church as soon as she stood up to preach – there was nothing she could do. Some could not get beyond her physical appearance as a woman, which defined her as a "non-priest" in their eyes.

*** ANNETTE'S MIXED BAG ***

Annette has been a pastoral associate for nine years. On the whole, she calls these years a wonderful and positive experience. She has the great privilege of working with a dynamic, collaborative pastor who recognized gifts she never knew she had. In spite of being total opposites in personality, Annette reports, they work well together. They have known each other for almost ten years. He encouraged her to apply for the lay formation program in the diocese. He is a great believer in adult education in the faith. A marvellous teacher, Annette's parish priest has taught theology in the program for many years.

"He teaches with authority and awakens a desire in his students to learn even more," she says. "He is largely responsible for calling forth gifts from me that I never knew I possessed. In addition, he has encouraged me to continue my studies in the Master of Divinity program now."

But Annette reports that not all testing has been positive. At one point, a young assistant pastor was assigned to the parish. He resented Annette's friendship and collaborative ministry with the pastor and did his best to undermine the relationship. In fact, he played them against each other.

> It was a very tense time for all of us. I thought the problem existed between the two pastors and I was trying not to get drawn into it. I learned later, however, that the assistant pastor wanted the pastor to fire me. All this was news to me! The situation was resolved when the assistant pastor was reassigned elsewhere. At one point, I offered to leave my position because I thought the pastor needed him more than me. The pastor refused, indicating that he needed a team to work with him and he doubted that this individual would ever be a team player.

I marvelled at Annette's capacity to regard even those who treat her less respectfully as people who are also in need of love and care.

> Certainly, I have encountered some male chauvinists among both clergy and laity. However, I always try to co-operate with them. I am very much a people person and I like harmony. I realize that not everyone is going to like me for whatever reason, so I try not to take things personally. I have learned that the more aggressive people are, often the lower the self-esteem they possess.

*** MARLENE'S PICTURE ***

Marlene paints a very different picture.

> The fact of being a female role model in leadership in a church of male leaders tests my call. It is an ongoing frustration to see people, by virtue of their maleness, being allowed to do bad ministry, to starve communities of the faith formation and support they hunger for.

Because Marlene's ministry takes her to a number of parishes, she finds adjusting to the pastors a real test. At the same time, the community of faith itself – at the parish, diocesan and academic levels – tests her call. A privatized or consumer approach to faith fostering a certain suspicion of learning and a general lack of interest in understanding Catholic faith and spirituality are attitudes found in many parishioners.

Being invited to teach and minister is a crucial element of having my call recognized and tested. When this does not happen, it is easy to get discouraged and wonder whether there are more satisfying ways to earn a living outside the Church.

I sigh. Carla, Annette and Marlene have said it well. The attitude of the ordained pastor can determine to a large extent our sense of affirmation, testing or even rejection. I can recall instances of all three.

As Annette has already observed, much seems to depend on a level of personal wholeness, maturity and integrity in the ordained pastor. His ability to affirm and respect the call and gifts of lay ecclesial ministers, and to work collaboratively with lay colleagues in pastoral ministry, especially women, can make or break our ministerial identity and experience of ministry. There is also a direct correlation between the community's understanding of Church and leadership, and this community's acceptance and rejection of a lay ecclesial minister.

*** CHAPLAINCY EXPERIENCE ***

One of the most affirming experiences of Audrey's work as a lay minister has been in the Clinical Pastoral Education (CPE) training she took for three years, before and during the time she was a full-time hospital chaplain. Audrey worked alongside and under the supervision of very fine, committed, highly skilled clergy – men and women – mostly from other Christian traditions. Each one acclaimed her as being as competent, professional and able as they were. Audrey learned and worked as an equal among equals. Doctors, nurses and health-care professionals appreciated her perspective as a chaplain, inviting her to accompany them to family meetings with their patients.

Once, a palliative care doctor, after assessing a patient, spoke first to me of the assessment, and suggested that I was in the best position to help this patient and the family. All of this has affirmed and legitimized my call to ministry, and I am most grateful for the affirmation both within and without, which fuels my commitment.

*

From my own difficult experiences, I have learned that trials and setbacks are the true test of the authenticity of one's call. It is precisely in experiences of rejection and judgment, often at the hands of professional church people, that I have found myself in a crucible of discernment. I have been haunted by self-doubt and fear. I have wondered if I knew how to love, how to serve, even how to discern. At such disintegration points, the fire in my heart – to serve God in ministry – would only intensify rather than being extinguished. Just when such despair seemed to collapse my ability and desire, a word, a look, a person's touch, an opportunity would appear, parting clouds of pain and despair, as if to say, "I am still out there and I am still calling you."

3

Nourishing the Spirit

[Christ] constantly makes available in his body, which is the church, gifts of ministries through which, by his power, we provide each other with the helps needed for salvation so that, doing the truth in love, we may in all things grow into him who is our head.

(Lumen Gentium, 9)

Your word is a lamp to my feet and a light to my path.

(Psalm 119:105)

I was in a bad state. I had been dismissed from a pastoral ministry position I loved deeply, a casualty of the parish's internal strife and politics. Under normal circumstances, I loved praying with the Scriptures. But during this painful time, I was in no mood to turn to God's Word. Why? Because I felt shame, and I fully expected to feel mocked and abandoned by those same Scriptures that at other times had been such a source of comfort and inspiration. No need to add insult to injury this time, Lord. I wanted to avoid the Word, preferring instead to wallow in grief, anger, disbelief and fear about my future.

Only days after my job ended, the editor of a liturgy publication asked me to write Scripture commentaries for several Sundays. I reluctantly agreed, realizing I had to earn a living somehow (what a noble reason to accept the writing assignment!). Perhaps this task would provide a little healing balm on the wound of rejection. Then something akin to a miracle happened. Despite my emotional resistance, the assignment forced me to spend considerable time with God's Word. As I allowed the words from Scripture to touch my pain, one thing became crystal clear: God would not have me buried in a tomb of despair, but used every crack in my sorrow to shine some consoling light into my soul.

*** ANNETTE'S PRAYER ***

This experience of healing through Scripture was a revelation, a consolation and a source of unending strength and love. And so when I listened to Annette, I knew from the inside about the power of God's Word that she describes.

> I pray with Scripture daily (liturgy of the hours and readings of the day). As a cantor and lector I proclaim the readings in the worshipping assembly. As I become more and more familiar with Scripture, it forms a stronger core within me. It forms me from the inside out. The passages that I have become familiar with over time are made available to me throughout the day. On days when my energy is low and I resist God's call, or when I doubt if I am in the right place, Jeremiah's experience of being called (Jeremiah 1:4-8) echoes through my spirit. I hum psalms and chant phrases and recall verses. I spend much time pondering the layers of meaning that a passage contains. Even the same words speak to me in different ways depending on what is happening in my life.

The notion that God's Word contains layers of meaning became clear to me when I started to approach the Word in preparation for preaching. Ardent study and prayer would often reveal many possible directions that a given sermon could take; yet I could choose only one or two if I didn't want to cause mental indigestion in those who would hear it. I learned that even a few holy words had the power to feed the soul over and over again.

*** GLADYS and SILENCE ***

Those in ministry discover an especially rich potential in Scripture for grounding their calling and their daily ministry. In her role as a parish pastoral leader in northern Canada, Gladys lives in close relationship to the Scriptures. The isolation from mainstream society and from the usual types of support pushed Gladys into the Scriptures with a special urgency and need.

First Nations people are much more comfortable with silence than people from European cultures are. For First Nations people, silence in the presence of others communicates respect rather than awkwardness, patience rather than not knowing what to say. This cultural value of silence taught Gladys to grow comfortable with regular times of solitary prayer with the Scriptures. She tries to live out her life, ministry and vocation with the following two Scripture passages: "You will love God, love your neighbour and love yourself" and "Whatsoever you do to the least of these, you do to me." Both these passages help Gladys to ground her life in what God has called her to do so she can properly live out her ministry and be the embodied response to people's needs.

> When you live in a small, isolated community where everyone knows you and knows what you do for a living, expectations are placed on you. I try to live the Scriptures in my actions and how I treat people. I truly believe that we teach best by what we do and not by what we say. So I try to live out the Scriptures in my daily life and point people to them for guidance, comfort and inspiration.

*

Sometimes the basis for doing ministry feels incredibly tenuous. If I can fall back on a formal mandate, it's not so bad. But if a formal mandate is missing, I grope in the dark for direction and even permission of sorts. At times I have been approached by strangers with a request to "do a funeral" outside of any official ministerial role. At other times I have found myself in a position where I was forced to defend or justify my ministry, in particular to ordained clergy or other leaders of the institutional Church. At such times, God's Word becomes particularly important as a source of strength, direction and mandate.

*** DEANNA'S JOURNEY ***

Deanna's description of Scripture as her "partner in crime" resonated deeply in me, even though, in her case, this phrase carries an unintended pun: Deanna works in prison ministry.

> Scripture forms the core of my personal prayer and leads the way to my journey with God, a journey of the heart. I preach on the Scriptures to the inmates in prison and I speak boldly about God and Jesus. Prison environment is a sexualized world, and as a woman chaplain I have to be very astute and tuned in to these dynamics, confronting them without backing away.
>
> Most of the inmates have never experienced a woman like me. When I smile at them or am friendly with them, they immediately interpret this in sexual ways. I have to be very explicit and explain that these gestures can also mean other things, like helping them feel better about themselves and reflecting the love of God for them. I am forever using Scripture to illustrate these things, and I feel totally protected by God – I feel that Scripture plays a significant role in this protection.

In the early days after my dismissal from parish ministry, I wept and wailed every time I approached the Scriptures. With the psalmist, I flung my pain against the Word of God. After I spend several prayer times in tears, God broke through, connecting my experience to Jesus himself.

As Jesus had wept over Jerusalem and its inability to embrace new life, I wept over the parish and over myself.

As Jesus was rejected by people in his hometown, I was dismissed from ministry in a parish close to home.

As Jesus was sacrificed to calm a nation, I felt sacrificed to maintain the status quo.

As Jesus forgave his executioners for not knowing what they were doing, so Jesus invited me to forgive the power brokers in the parish, for they truly had no idea what they had done.

As Jesus instructed his disciples, so he instructed me to shake off the dust from my feet when I was no longer welcome.

The connections forged with Jesus shattered my sense of isolation and abandonment. There now truly was one who stood by me and with me, for clearly he had gone before me in all things. Those connections became the rope God threw to me to rescue me from despair. This despair took a long time to lift, but it never quite swallowed me up, thanks to the holy Word, a living Word that gives life in all circumstances.

*** MILLIE'S DECISION ***

The Word of God is truly alive and active. Not only does it offer consolation in times of sorrow, it also helps guide us in important decisions, as Millie explains so well.

> After a time away from the parish, working more in high school ministry and in hospital ministry, I felt again the pull to return to the parish. When I was offered the parish where I presently serve, though I had expressed interest, I nevertheless lived through a very heart-wrenching and soul-searching week before I finally accepted.
>
> The many affirming parts of being a woman in ministry came to me, but so did the loneliness, the isolation, the not being part of the "boys' club," the "24/7" dimension of the work. They all came up in my being, as did the many tasks that no one knows or cares about – it was a painful jumble in my heart. My greatest and most enduring impetus to work in this ministry came from Isaiah: "The Spirit of the Lord is upon me, for He has anointed me" (61:1-2). What finally helped me say yes was drawn from the resurrection account of Jesus' dialogue with Peter – "Feed my lambs" and "feed my sheep" – in John 21, and especially the paraphrased words that follow: "When you were young you did your own thing, but now that you are older…you will go where you would rather not go."

*

sParish ministry is a real eye-opener. The biggest issue lurking in the background is always self-care. I don't know how priests survive year after year doing this job, with very little support and very little nurturing of their spirits. This is the ideal place for burnout, and I am always conscious of that. The example of Jesus in the Scriptures challenges me to take self-care seriously; many times Jesus withdrew to pray.

Jesus knew that only God, the only one who is infinite, is capable of satisfying the infinite hunger for love. It is God's love alone that sustains healthy pastoral ministry. To continue giving of himself, Jesus needed to withdraw and re-centre. In withdrawing, he drank from the well who is God, becoming free to love and to forgive unconditionally.

Jesus also withdrew to meet his own need, especially in the midst of his own struggles – his prayer in Gethsemane is the most poignant example of this. Jesus did not feel guilty about his doubts, nor did he ignore his fear. He did not pretend to have everything under control. He simply offered the raw terror in his own heart. Up to three times he offered God his fear. It was in that very process of handing over his terror that God reached out and strengthened him.

Being called to walk with God's people, I can do no less than pattern my ministry on Jesus himself. An active prayer life sustains me and keeps me anchored. It also increases communion with people in need. It is an interesting exercise to pray with an experience of rejection and invisibility as a means of solidarity with the countless people in the world whose gifts are not appreciated, whose hard work is not noticed, and who are not empowered to pursue their dreams.

Prayer always creates community, uniting our hearts to one another and to God, even if the pain is too deep for words, even if ministry exhausts us, even if at times all we have to offer is a broken spirit and eyes red from crying, and more questions than answers.

Sometimes I am called upon simply to share someone's grief, even to keep the faith on behalf of one who seems incapable of keeping the faith herself. At other times I'm the one who needs the loving embrace of another. For the sake of self-care, I foster a strong support network among family, friends and colleagues from various faith backgrounds. I have known times when my faith in God, myself and the world was so weak that others have had to watch over me. I need to be honest and humble enough to know when it is time for me to reach out to those who love me and care for me.

*** FRANCINE'S FOCUS ***

Francine explained her practice of focusing her prayer on the icon of the Saviour of Zvenigorod (Rublev), which she has placed in a prominent place in her living room.[8] It shows Jesus' face and shoulders, slightly turned. The icon appears slightly damaged, with some sections missing on both top and bottom. Henri Nouwen, in *Behold the Beauty of the Lord*, says that for him, the facial expression of Jesus in this icon became a profound spiritual experience: the Saviour does not look severe; he doesn't judge, but simply sees everything. For Francine, the image of Jesus portrayed in that icon is one of the most engaging, rich and profound seen anywhere: "It leads one to contemplate the mystery of Jesus as Compassion of God, Word of the Father, Truth, Justice and Mercy, Suffering Servant, Bearer of all, Soul Friend, Beloved." Each time she gazes upon the image, it says something new to her. "Jesus has been a companion and guide for many, many years. It's a relationship that grows and deepens," she reflects.

At the same time, when Francine teaches Christology in the lay formation program of her diocese, she can be fairly academic in her presentation. She does not consider these two approaches as divorced from one another, but as a sign that her relationship with Jesus is unique and personal, just as every other person's is. She adds, "I hope what comes through in my teaching and in my prayer is that one area informs and forms the other. As my understanding of Jesus grows, so too does my relationship."

*

My own spirit is nourished through the liturgy, in particular the Eucharist. As Vatican II stated, the Eucharist is the "source and summit of our Christian life."[9] I believe this with my whole heart. I believe God feeds us with Christ's sacramental body and blood in the Eucharist in order for us to go out and be Eucharist to a world hungry for God. For me, the liturgy, with "full, conscious and active participation"[10] by everyone, along with good music and sound preaching, feeds soul and spirit like nothing else on earth possibly can.

Besides finding primary nourishment in the Eucharist and in a life-giving support network among family and friends, I engage in regular private prayer and meditation, spiritual reading, taking workshops, making a yearly retreat, and much reflecting in solitude – some of the food groups in a diet that nourishes the spirit.

*** MARLENE'S MODEL ***

Intentional about connecting with significant women in the Bible, Marlene identifies very strongly with Mary Magdalene. As Marlene puts it, "She was called by Jesus, accompanied him and was commissioned by him to spread the Gospel. She had a unique relationship with him, and he taught her things that the others just wouldn't get." Throughout Christian history, Mary Magdalene has been confused with other women in the Gospels, notably the woman caught in adultery in John 8:1-11. Fortunately, recent research and biblical scholarship is correcting this error, and is now restoring her prominence as the first witness to the resurrection, the one called by the risen Christ to "go and tell" the disciples that he had risen. In the early Church, Mary Magdalene bore the title "Apostle to the apostles."[11]

Marlene points out that the Gnostic Gospel of Mary tells us that Mary Magdalene had friends, followers and supporters. Some people resented this. Marlene sees her as intelligent, wise and courageous. "I may not have all the same attributes," she tells me, "but it is with that image and model that I identify most strongly."

*

Sometimes praying with Scripture sustains us for a long time. When I have been uncertain about where God is leading me, Jeremiah 29:11-14 consoles and guides me at the most unexpected times: "For surely I know the plans I have for you, says the Lord, plans for your welfare and not for harm, to give you a future with hope." When I have felt saddened and grieved over limitations placed upon my ministry,

Matthew's Beatitudes come to life: "Blessed are those who mourn, for they will be comforted" (5:4).

*** GLADYS'S IMAGE ***

Gladys has had similar experiences with Scripture.

> A composite image from Scripture came to me during a Bible study of Genesis 2 several decades ago. I saw God as a hand, first outstretched like Michelangelo's hands of God and Adam on the ceiling of the Sistine Chapel, then through Jeremiah's "clay in the potter's hands," forming, moulding, and sometimes having to press down and reform the clay. This was followed by Isaiah's promise of God holding me "in the palm of my hand," culminating finally in Christ's parable of the gardener pruning the plants, removing that which is stunting growth, sometimes painfully, so that new life can come forth.

This image continues to have a rich and powerful effect on Gladys. It consoles her in times of distress, it challenges her in times of doubt and fear, and it reflects to her what ministry is meant to be. Gladys sees in this image that she is called to be ever open to the creating and recreating hand of God, a hand that comforts, challenges and points the way.

> My ministry is always changing and adapting to the situations and people God calls me to. I need to be open to the challenges and possibilities God offers me, while staying aware of God's hand in my life and ministry.

*** TEAMWORK ***

Wylma and Darlene work together in pastoral ministry to First Nations people in an urban setting, with some pastoral responsibilities for several reserve parishes in the area. Last year, William, a deacon, joined them. The three of them share a communal life, prepare children and adults for sacraments and, assisted by volunteers, operate a clothing depot.

*** DARLENE'S VISIONS ***

Darlene is somewhat reluctant when I ask how Scripture nourishes her spirit. Finally, she shares that her prayer experiences are not all that conventional – am I certain that I wish to include them? This only intrigues me more. When I respond affirmatively, Darlene explains.

During a 30-day retreat many years ago, I heard a line from a poem spoken aloud to me as I prayed: "Come live with me and be my love." Those words changed my understanding of myself in relation to Jesus and to others. I know that it is not my activity but the quality of my presence that is of primary importance in ministry. Because I live with Jesus in the presence of the Father and animated by the Holy Spirit, I can actually be his love to others. I know from experience that this means that as I listen, Jesus listens, bringing hope and effecting healing, even when others are least aware of it. I know that where I walk, Jesus also walks with me pointing out those who need my attention.

During a retreat before beginning my current ministry, again I heard a line that shapes all I do: "Show my people that I love them." The people I minister to are marginalized within the Church. I have always experienced the Church as being far greater than the body of those who come together to worship. The Mystical Body has been very real to me since my childhood. So even though I experience being marginalized because of being a woman in ministry, and because I work within the Aboriginal community, I feel a very real connection to the Church.

In another prayer experience I found myself in a church during a liturgy, where the bishop and priests were all gathered around the altar. The congregation was praying and singing. Then I turned around and saw that the whole back wall of the church was gone, and, at the back, people were coming and going, carrying on with their daily lives. And I was told: "This is my Church." I understood that daily life and liturgical celebration are two parts of one whole. Jesus is present among all those who cannot access liturgy, and even to those who do not know they are walking with him.

*** WYLMA'S HOME ***

The single scripture quote that speaks most to Wylma is John 15:4 in the Jerusalem Bible translation: "Make your home in me as I make mine in you." This is more commonly translated as "Abide in me as I abide in you," or "Remain in me, and I will remain in you." The verse continues, "As a branch cannot bear fruit all by itself, but must remain part of the vine, neither can you unless you remain in me."

For Wylma, the second part of this verse is a description of ministry within the Body of Christ. For a very long time, probably several years, whenever she went to pray, this scripture would surface within her and all she could do was stay with it. In a very real and deep way, it captures the essence of her vocation and role in the Church, now lived out in ministry to First Nations people.

> The core concept of Jesus Christ being at home in me, and I in him, summarizes the context of my ministry. It is not only what I do, but who I am, that makes a difference to people. When others speak to me I can be confident that Christ is listening, and that he is doing the healing. When I speak, as long as I intend to be faithful to him, I can be confident that he is allowing the right words to be said, and that he will see to their effectiveness.

Wylma muses on the word "home" in the Jerusalem Bible translation, because it connotes at-home-ness, a sense of the family hearth. She sees many people who are lonely, who feel empty, without a spiritual home; they are hurting and lost. Wylma knows she does not need to "fix" their lives, but, she says,

> I do need to allow them to draw near to the Christ who is in me, so that he can minister to them. In my ministry I believe, and find experientially, that relationship has a huge priority over function. Christ's at-home-ness in me allows me to have a partnership and community with him that is at the core of my ministry. I believe that there are many in the Church who live this reality without necessarily articulating it.

*

When God placed me on this journey in ministry, I responded swiftly with a Jeremiah-like objection: "Don't call me, Lord, I am only a Catholic woman." I admit that I have been reluctant, defiant and disbelieving. Yet none of this has stopped God from lighting the fire of service for ministry in my heart. Fear and self-doubt have been overcome by intimate encounters with the risen Jesus, making me go out into places of ministry, boldly announcing with Mary Magdalene, "I have seen the Lord!" (John 20:18).

Experiences of affirmation had me exclaim with the disciples, "Lord, even the demons submit to us!" (Luke 10:17). As he did with the disciples, Jesus would gently adjust my perspective. "Do not rejoice that the spirits submit to you, but rejoice that your names are written in heaven" (Luke 10:20). Such experiences were followed by rejection, painful betrayal and exclusion, sometimes at the hands of "good" church people. At those times God pushed me deeper into the Gospels: Jesus weeping over Jerusalem, Jesus feeling betrayed by Peter, Jesus crying out that "they know not what they do."

When I have found myself facing new challenges in ministry and I have been afraid and worried, the apostle Paul has been right beside me: "We have this treasure in clay jars, so that it may be made clear that this extraordinary power belongs to God and does not come from us" (2 Cor 4:7). "My grace is sufficient for you, for power is made perfect in weakness" (2 Cor 12:9). And when unusual opportunities for ministry have opened up by surprise, the Scriptures once again have reminded me that God's Spirit makes no distinction. "There is no longer Jew or Greek, slave or free, male and female; for all are one in Christ Jesus" (Gal 3:28).

My spirit drinks deeply from the Holy Word, ensuring that I do not walk alone in any aspect of this ministry journey. I feel like leaven in the bread of Christ's Body, the Church: "The kingdom of heaven is like yeast that a woman took and mixed in with three measures of flour until all of it was leavened" (Matthew 13:33). As God's Word in Scripture penetrates my lived experience, it leaps off the pages of the Bible and acts in my heart much like yeast in bread. That living relationship with Scripture has become an essential core of my spiritual nourishment in good times and bad, of my direction for ministry, and of the authority that grounds that ministry.

*** SACRAMENTS AND PRAYER ***

For women in ministry, praying with Scripture and participating in the sacraments of the Church become sources of living water in our relationship to Jesus and in our ministry. We burn with a desire to share this rich source of water with others. One of the hardest things to face is other people's apparent indifference to discovering and turning to this source of living water, especially in those who do attend church. Take the celebration of the Eucharist. Gladys reflects.

> The Mass *is* our lives as Catholic Christians, and I see this more and more. I encourage people to get to Mass, but still have not found how to help them to *want* to be there. For those who do come, I appreciate their presence – a sign that we are not alone on our faith journey. It is difficult and often seems impossible to get people to gather at other times in the week for faith sharing or preparing the Sunday liturgy. One young girl has been leading the singing for the past two years. I try to practise with her each week. As for readers, I can only ask people as they arrive before Mass. Lists do not work because people will not promise to be present on a given Sunday.

Many women working in ministry are closely involved with the sacraments. Women are the front-line catechists preparing adults and children to receive and celebrate the sacraments of baptism, confirmation, Eucharist and marriage. Through such intimate involvement we discover the depth and beauty of these sacraments and how they contribute to our spiritual development. Not to find a similar interest and hunger among the faithful whom we serve grieves and discourages us.

*

As I hear Gladys share her experiences in parish ministry, I recall an experience of my own that reveals similar regrets. At a social gathering with other Catholic couples, several bemoaned their inability to experience God in church and through the sacraments. The upshot of the conversation was a severe criticism of the Church for being an obstacle to, rather than a vehicle for, nourishing their faith.

The conversation focused in particular on the celebration of the Eucharist and the sacrament of reconciliation. I listened quietly for a while before I finally offered some of my very positive experiences of both these sacraments. I emphasized the truism that "you get out of it what you put into it." I spoke in particular about the connection I feel between my preaching ministry and sacramental confession. I shared how my need for the sacrament of reconciliation has increased with the exercising of the public ministry of preaching.

Judging from their blank looks, I was unsure whether my friends could hear past their own woundedness and frustrations with the institutional Church. They struggled to find in the Church's sacramental celebrations any connection with their own lives. In turn, the Church's mechanical, almost minimalist, celebration of sacraments did not put my friends in touch with the deep life-giving power of the sacramental life. They ached to have the homily help them to connect the challenges of modern life with the timeless Word of God; they often leave with spirits unfed. Too many experiences with weak and inadequate pastoral leadership have left these friends discouraged about the future vitality of their parishes.

I realized anew the importance of spiritual freedom, a gift that helps us to drink deeply from the Church's sacramental wellsprings. Institutional legalism and prohibitions, poor liturgy and leadership do not have to have the power to imprison my spirit, a spirit whose freedom can be rooted in God alone.

*** INSTRUMENTS OF GRACE ***

Gladys is right when she states that negative attitudes toward the sacraments can be found anywhere, including in her northern parishioners. "Personally, it is very important for me to have a regular confessor," she explains. "The priest is available before Mass on Wednesday and Sunday – few people seem to take advantage of the opportunity. Generally, reconciliation does not seem to be valued or understood."

Gladys noted that many families request baptism for their infants. To accommodate the demand, she formed a baptism preparation team with two women from the parish, but they lost interest after one year. Using diocesan guidelines and good catechetical materials, she prepared couples who wished to have children baptized. She tried to help them understand the centrality of the Eucharist. But on more than one occasion, at the family's request and with very short notice, the priest baptized children who had had no preparation.

> When we prepare children for Confirmation and First Communion, the people may show enthusiasm in the months leading up to the completion of initiation, but the number of families who continue to participate each week is almost zero. We have a few children who attend regularly on their own – never do their parents or guardians accompany them. Those children inspire me very much.

Given these kinds of challenges, pastoral ministry can often feel like the work of the baker woman mixing her yeast into three measures of flour. We serve in ministry because of God's call, but our efforts seem to disappear in the larger scheme and, like yeast that disappears in the dough, we do not see immediate results from our labour. At times we wonder about the leavening qualities of the yeast we contribute through our faithful and faith-filled service. We stick with it because it is the fullest expression of who we have become in Christ. We stick with it because ministry has become for us the pearl of great price, a pearl that gives us the fullness of life that God wishes for all people.

Scripture feeds our spirit and personal prayer grounds our personal identity in God. The sacraments connect us to Jesus in concrete nourishment and the liturgy joins us to others as we praise and thank God, as we offer our needs to God and give ourselves in service to God. This food for the soul gives us the patient perseverance to be faithful to our calling in ministry.

*** ANNETTE'S PASSION ***

Annette's main areas of ministry involve music, liturgy and sacramental preparation with children and adults. She defines her calling in this way.

I am a liturgist. The liturgy and its music are my passion. I want to study liturgy more. In fact, I want to preside at liturgy. I have been able to do so at non-Eucharistic liturgies like funeral vigils and services of the Word. As far as sacraments go, it gives me great joy to prepare people for the sacraments, especially in RCIA and baptism preparation. I want to share my passion and experience of the sacraments with others, and I wish I could actually celebrate some of the sacraments as presider.

*

Parish pastoral ministry requires a deep spiritual and prayer discipline. The never-ending demands of meetings and workshops, teaching and preaching (whatever form this takes), and the pastoral needs of individual parishioners can be met only if I remain solidly grounded in God through solitude and prayer. Fostering inner freedom disposes me to relate to parishioners from that place inside where neither my own sinfulness, nor my own woundedness, nor my personal agendas rule my interactions and perceptions.

I have witnessed parish meetings where interactions among the participants were permeated with unresolved and unacknowledged tensions, anger and grief. Walking with parishioners in such circumstances demands not only integrity, but a deep and intense prayer life. The prevalence of human brokenness in most parishes can trap one into feeling compelled to "fix" people. Yet ministry is more about being a calm and healing presence amid the brokenness than about a comprehensive repair plan. It is in and through the quality of the pastoral presence that God heals and restores. Prayer and solitude are therefore essential to keep my perspectives clear, my own pet peeves under wraps, and my spiritual, emotional and mental energy replenished. Striking a balance between my active pastoral work and my need for solitude and prayer remains a huge challenge. However, finding the balance is crucial to the quality of my presence as a pastoral minister.

You are the salt of the earth; but if salt has lost its taste, how can its saltiness be restored? It is no longer good for anything, but is thrown out and trampled under foot. You are the light of the world. A city built on a hill cannot be hid. No one after lighting a lamp puts it under the bushel basket, but on the lamp stand, and it gives light to all in the house. In the same way, let your light shine before others, so that they may see your good works and give glory to your Father in heaven. (Matthew 5:13-16)

*** NOURISHING THE SPIRIT ***

Darlene has made praying a way of living each day. She nourishes her spirit by constant prayer – in season and out! She also points out the advantage of team ministry and how this enriches her prayer life.

> I feel fortunate to have Wylma and William – we pray as a community several times a day. The knowledge that I am where God wants me, doing the work he wants done each day, is what sustains me through difficult times, and gifts me with perseverance. I receive hope and courage from the response of the people I deal with each day.

Wylma nourishes her spirit by praying with the daily Mass readings each morning and by participating in community prayer (Morning Prayer or Mass or both), either with her ministry partners or in the parish church. But praying is larger than this for Wylma. She regards enjoying life and using the talents that she has been given as a form of prayer.

> I love walking and never tire of the beauty that surrounds us. I get a lot of energy from creating things like stories, poems, cards, crafts. Whenever there is a chance for dancing, I take it and feel rejuvenated by the music and the exercise. I enjoy research and study so my spirit is refreshed by various projects.

At the diocesan level, Wylma gets nourishment from meeting with others in ministry, and she has participated on a number of committees that stimulated and encouraged her. She often attends workshops. Some of these are nourishing; others are a challenge, especially when individuals are locked in bitterness.

The First Nations people who are most negative to Wylma have nearly always come from other communities and do not know her personally. "They seem to equate me with an uncaring institutional

Church and/or other non-Natives who have not dealt respectfully with First Nations people," she explains.

*

Whether our spirit's nourishment comes from Scripture, support from colleagues (ordained and lay), retreats and workshops, spiritual reading, private and communal prayer, spiritual direction or the sacraments, these resources require our personal initiative before they become part of our spiritual diet. Whereas many dioceses have built-in supports for their priests – such as annual priests' retreats and conferences, funding for retreats and sabbaticals – in most dioceses, lay ecclesial ministers cannot access such supports. There is no funding available for our initial study and formation (except for bursaries from a few religious orders), nor for continuing education or sabbaticals.

Many of us can only be employed in ministry and take part in workshops, retreats and continuing forms of education because we have access to private financial resources that pay for these things, most notably spouses who earn a decent income. The family's financial and emotional support thus provides a unique contribution to the Church, a contribution that often remains invisible.

The nature and demands of pastoral ministry require us to take responsibility for our ongoing personal growth and prayer. No amount of diocesan or spousal support can take the place of our own willingness to find ways to grow in our relationship to God through Jesus Christ. It is only in our daily surrender to God's calling, seeking healing and forgiveness, sacramentally and otherwise, that we can become open channels of God's grace to others. Neither priests nor lay ecclesial ministers can be in the business of providing ministry if we ourselves are not also committed to receiving ministry, whether that be through Scripture, spiritual direction and prayer, the sacraments and spiritual formation, or ongoing study and formation. Walking our talk is part of our call.

After a particularly challenging number of days on the road and in the air – doing workshops, a parish mission and pulpit supply, each in a different community – I returned home. I had taught, preached, listened, led worship and prayed with many. Each encounter was holy and fed my spirit immeasurably. My gratitude and praise for the God who calls me to minister was swift and generous, but I was exhausted. I felt the fragility of the clay jar that is my person, in which God's grace has chosen to dwell. My lakeside farm home served as the refuge where I could withdraw and regroup in the safety of my primary relationships of love, with my husband and with God. Jesus gently invited me into sacred solitude in my heart.

> That evening, at sundown, they brought to Jesus all who were sick or possessed with demons. And the whole city was gathered around the door. […] In the morning, while it was still very dark, Jesus got up and went out to a deserted place, and there he prayed. (Mark 1:32, 35)

4

Called and Commissioned

Then there are those lay persons chosen by God who are called by the bishop to give themselves fully to apostolic works and who labour very fruitfully in the Lord's field.

(Lumen Gentium, 41)

"Who told you that you can just do this?" That question again! Every time I step into a Catholic pulpit to preach, the eyes of some listeners reveal this question in their hearts. The question can colour hearing and obstruct trust. All I can do is pray for hearts to be open to conversion. Sometimes it happens: "I didn't know women could preach!" For others, suspicion and a refusal to accept keep ears and hearts closed. For them, the Word of God returns empty, and I grieve.

Carla faced "the question" in an angry parishioner who objected to a major decision: "By what authority do you claim the right to make such a decision?" Millie's bishop had to answer a similar question at a diocesan meeting: "How can you claim that a lay person has authority in the parish, when canon law clearly states that the pastor is the head of the parish?" Sharon was questioned at the grocery store one day while standing in line at the check-out: "So, do you think you can make all the decisions in the parish?"

Even if we believe deep in our hearts that we have a vocation, that God calls us to exercise ministry in the Church, this alone is not sufficient to validate what we do. "What makes you think God called you?" Questions such as these abound for newcomers in ministry, especially women. And rightly so. As noted earlier, the very nature of ministry revolts against a freelance marketing approach. The heart and purpose of ministry revolt against privatization. Just because we experience God's call to ministry, this alone is not enough to give us licence to practice. God indeed calls individuals, but this call is not intended for the individual. In order to be activated and to be effective, the call must be verified, recognized, "authorized" by the community of faith.

Ideally, three sources of authority intersect to form the mandate for service in pastoral ministry: an inner call, affirmation by the faith community, and an ecclesiastical endorsement. This chapter explores the aspect of authority for women in ministry. How does the community recognize and affirm a woman's vocation? What constitutes the community's authority? And how is the authority expressed and exercised?

*** SHARON'S INNER CALL ***

Sharon leans forward, a gesture alerting me that she acknowledges the importance of the question and she's focusing her thoughts.

> The initial inner call was there when I was young, but life circumstances forced me to put it aside. Yet it was never far from the surface, making itself felt as a beckoning, a desire that was fuelled by small things: prayer, liturgy, the sacraments, teaching the kids catechism, wanting to be explicit about my faith in the workplace, aching to serve God in the Church. Then came Fr. John — he recognized my gifts, entrusted me with ministry tasks, boosted my self-confidence, challenged me to learn, to study, and to grow in my faith. Fr. John invited my ideas and perspectives on things, and he listened.

*

The inner call is elusive, yet tangible. All my own "firsts" come to mind:

The first time I led worship, I was both nervous and comfortable at the same time.

The first time I preached, the pulpit felt strange and familiar.

The first time I provided pastoral care to a grieving family, and subsequently led the funeral service, produced both apprehension and a surprising satisfaction.

The first time I faced conflict in a parish where I worked, the challenging task of opening communication in love brought both peace and courage.

And the first time I preached a retreat, spoke at a conference, facilitated a workshop I experienced strong feelings of newness and a coming home to what is right for me: to be a witness, a teacher, a guide.

This strange combination of experiencing something utterly new with a deep sense of the familiar is often the first indication of an inner calling. For me, each of these firsts was accompanied not only by external fruits (affirmation from the faith community), but also by internal growth: my relationship to Jesus deepened, my insights into the Scriptures developed, my affection for the Church grew and my desire to serve God's people increased. As my passion was tapped, my true calling was awakened, desire grew, and a reservoir of unbounded energy, creativity and vision opened in my mind, heart and soul.

*** DEANNA'S HEALING JOURNEY ***

Before Deanna engages "the question," she quips about her rapport with the inmates. "I have fewer problems with my authority in prison than I had in the parish!" Then her voice lowers as she goes back into her memories. When Deanna embarked on the long healing journey with God, several stops on the way helped awaken her inner call.

> The Alcoholics Anonymous (AA) 12 Steps introduced me to a loving God; the charismatic Christians introduced me to Scripture and the Holy Spirit. Through both these doors I was led into an intimate relationship with Jesus. My approach to liturgy, ministry, sacraments, Church and community flows from this. And my relationship with God through Jesus in the Holy Spirit in turn strengthens my inner authority to do what I do. I just go forth in faith, no strings attached, and things open up. The right people with ecclesiastical authority (bishop, chaplain, priests, nuns) come my way and doors are opened.

*** GLADYS'S FULFILLMENT ***

Gladys chuckles as she remembered fearing the truth of her inner call for such a long time.

> I'd run in all kinds of different directions seeking fulfillment. I had several jobs and relationships, travelled and tried different studies, even tried to be satisfied in being a trusted and devoted parish volunteer. I guess I had a gut feeling this call was all-encompassing and I wasn't ready to give it my all for a long time.

Once the truth of God's call is faced and responded to, the restlessness makes way for deep fulfillment accompanied by an intimate knowing of being in the right place at the right time, even if the actual work of ministry is demanding and unrelenting.

"The contentment I enjoy now is new," says Gladys. "This confirms beyond a shadow of a doubt that I am finally doing what I am called to do." We sit together in holy silence for a while, so conscious of the precious nature of this journey God prepared for us. What deep joy, to find unity between our doing and our being.

*

Because the scope of my ministry extends beyond one parish or workplace, I have felt acutely the importance of discerning the authenticity of God's call. My place of studies became a place of awakenings. Some of my teachers and fellow-students saw potential and callings that I was unaware of at first. "Have you considered ministry?" No, not really. I'm just here, taking a few courses in pastoral counselling. But as I voiced my reply, a new song was born in my heart. A new dream appeared on the horizon of my life. Questions and encouragement from others awakened dreams and painted vistas that were not outside but inside of me, yet I never knew it. But here they were, and no one was more surprised than I.

Once God's call was awakened and affirmed, there was no going back, despite surprise and anxiety. Working out a concrete expression of my call still required a lot of work and a focused listening with the heart. Developing the gifts and skills required to exercise the call to ministry fruitfully and responsibly required effort and study. The daunting task of how to bear fruit in ministry as a woman within the Roman Catholic Church only added to the challenge of developing an "obedience" – a deep listening – to God's voice. But as my ability to name, and to respond to, God's call increased, the doubting diminished. As I sharpened my listening of the heart in prayer and with trusted others, as I developed skills and gifts, there also developed a deep sense of coming home to myself, to who I am supposed to become in this life. True ministry requires that I be first of all true to my deepest self, and that is the peace I have found.

*** SHARON'S UNFOLDING ***

An authenticating mark of a call is definitely inside us, but that is only the beginning. Another, equally important, authenticating mark comes from outside of us. As we grow more fully into the person God is calling us to be, a servant in pastoral ministry, there is a corresponding recognition and response from the faith community. Sharon describes her experience.

> My involvement grew over time. A gradual unfolding from being a parish volunteer, to slowly being entrusted with more by both the community and by the pastor, to then becoming a pastoral associate, and now a pastoral parish administrator. This is the second parish in which I serve in this capacity. As I offered my gifts and abilities, the faith community responded by its affirmative reception.

The community of faith needs to recognize in the pastoral minister a person who is competent, trustworthy and credible. As we consider meeting the needs of parishioners as a sacred task, the possibility increases that our ministry will be recognized and endorsed.

*** LENORA'S JOY ***

Lenora looks to the faith community, and to the fruits of her ministry, as the source of affirmation and also of deep joy.

> My biggest joy is to see people grow and blossom through my ministry and, in turn, start to share their gifts with others. When others become passionate

about their faith, and the light goes on, and when their hunger for more learning increases, I feel both affirmed and authorized in my calling.

For Lenora, support from her spouse, relatives and friends contributes to the strengthening and legitimizing of her call into ministry. "Significant others function as a mirror; when they affirm what they see in me, I grow in trust and in my ability to surrender to this call to minister to God's people," she tells me.

*

Significant others always play a major role in the awakening of callings and gifts. For example, I never considered myself to be a good writer. Having been raised and educated in the Dutch language, I considered my proficiency in English to be mediocre at best, even though I enjoyed good marks for my high school English classes in the Netherlands.

Even the feedback I received for papers and essays written in my years of seminary studies did not convince me. When asked, "Do you know that you write very well?", I'd reply without hesitation, "Not possible; English is not my first language."

Once I started preaching, a fellow student asked, "Are you aware of the power of your words?" I replied, now sheepishly, "No. What do you mean?" I knew the power of preaching as it affected me, but I was partially blind to how my preaching affected my audience. Communications theory tells us of the mysterious alchemy that happens between the moment that words leave our lips and the moment these same words land in the hearts and minds of listeners. While I choose words with the intention to convey certain meanings, I cannot control the variables inside the listener as these words land in his or her spirit. Sometimes I intend one thing and the hearer receives something quite different. Power is unleashed when the listener's spirit is fed in ways unique to his or her needs at that time, and when somehow words carry that mysterious soul food both with my intended meaning and with the overflow of meaning added by the listener.

One day, after the usual exchange of the question "Do you know that you write well?" and my customary response, "Not possible," my friend retorted, "But it is precisely because English is not your first language that you're much more intentional in its use than many of us who were raised in the English language and got used to a sloppy use of words."

This was the first reply that made some sense to me. From then on I paid closer attention to my own linguistic process. I grew more capable of embracing the gift of writing, the gift and the power of words, and took greater responsibility in the ongoing development of the gift. In this entire process the feedback from others served as a significant mirror and sounding board. Many women recall a similar process that helped them to discover and appropriate their call to ministry.

*** DEANNA'S DISCOVERY ***

There are times and places when the affirmation from the faith community is problematic. Before Deanna worked in prison chaplaincy, she was a pastoral associate in a parish. She sees a marked difference between the two groups she has served in ministry. While she had turned her back on the secular culture when she re-entered the Christian faith, she discovered that the secular culture was alive and well in the pews and in parish dynamics.

"While I can speak openly with the inmates about God and Jesus, and the power of God's saving activity as I had experienced it so dramatically in my own life, parishioners didn't seem to be able to handle strong God-talk without labelling me as fanatic," she observed.

The bitterness and hurt in her voice do not escape me as she continues, "'Holy Mother Church' tells us that we are called to live holy lives, but according to some people in the parish, we're not supposed to show it or express it too strongly. Fellow Catholics often want to tone down any talk of God. That's an ironic contradiction, and it annoys me."

The inmates with whom Deanna works appreciate her for pulling no punches and for her blunt honesty with them. Ironically, Deanna experienced parishioners as shying away from her for these very same qualities.

*** SHARON'S SELF-UNDERSTANDING ***

Sometimes such pulling away is caused by a distrust of the role played by a lay ecclesial minister, especially if this is a new experience for parishioners. A clerical mentality still operates to varying degrees in most parishes. For centuries the Catholic reflex has regarded "Father" as the centre for the parish's liturgical ministry and pastoral responsibilities. Sharon recalls that when she was growing up, Father would come to dinner and everyone had to be on their best behaviour. "It was such an honour to have the priest come to our house, as if he was next to God," she adds. It is therefore no surprise that seeing a non-ordained person, who is also a woman, in places previously occupied by the priest can upset unconsciously held images, expectations and attitudes. "I feel I have to work harder at earning people's trust and respect," admits Sharon. "It doesn't come as automatically and blindly as it does for many priests."

She explains her self-understanding and what authorizes her role.

> As a leader, I feel it is essential that our people recognize that this is their church, not Father's church, and that the community is far more important than who the administrator happens to be. So often I find that our people leave their expertise and adult identity at the door when they enter the church. Vestiges of clericalism operate in both clergy and lay people. Whatever Father wants is okay, even if it is largely disruptive of the way the community functions.

I ask Sharon for some examples.

> In the first year of my being the parish administrator, there was no sacramental minister assigned. The parish was served by a variety of visiting priests. The second year, the parish was assigned a sacramental minister, and then, all of a sudden, people were back to asking, "But what does Father want?" It has been, and continues to be, a tough struggle to get people again and again to

claim their church as theirs and to get the priest to realize he is not in charge, but is to lead in service to the community.

*

It has not been part of the Catholic ethos that a parish community claim a certain ownership and responsibility for its pastoral and spiritual well-being. Even with the creation of parish pastoral councils, very few such councils move past the material and financial concerns. We're comfortable repairing the roof, but in spiritual and pastoral matters, "Father knows best."

One year I preached on a regular basis in a Lutheran congregation that was searching for a new pastor. Since the previous pastor had been there nearly ten years, the recommendation was that the congregation needed a year to take stock of its life as a faith community. Through regular meetings of the church council and the congregation at large, members assessed who they were as a faith community and what their unique strengths and weaknesses were. This was followed by a visioning process with short-term and long-term pastoral planning.

The findings from this process were then used to put together a profile of the kind of pastor this congregation needed at that time. It was only then that the actual search for a new minister began. While this process had its shortcomings, I was impressed by how it allowed parishioners to take ownership of the pastoral and spiritual quality of their life as a Christian family.

*** GLADYS'S DREAMS ***

Gladys dreams of each parishioner sharing the pastoral and spiritual responsibility to be a family of faith together. She has found that it is hard enough to awaken people's hunger for God, let alone have them take ownership to feed one another the spiritual food of the Gospel. Gladys tries to be creative in finding ways to tap into people's hunger for God and to offer them good nourishment. Gladys's preaching, working with young families and their children, preparing folks for the sacraments, and journeying with the dying and their families are all vehicles to offer people not only intellectual food, but a sense of spirituality and community as well.

"It always surprises and saddens me," she says, "when I hear that people don't come to church if there is no Mass. I always feel that celebrating the Word with Holy Communion is also real prayer with our family of faith, and I feel so affirmed by it."

*** SHARON'S SIGNS ***

Sharon never takes the acceptance of the faith community for granted.

> Some people in the faith community were shocked when I was named as their minister. Some never have got over it. Two, at least, have gone to another parish. One woman refuses to talk to me, though she still comes. However, just a few weeks ago, a "macho" man said, "You do the work of two priests – our parish has never had anything like this before!" This was an important affirmation that I am recognized in the community and accepted for who I am, and that is blessing.

*** FRANCINE'S VIEW ***

For Francine, authorization operates on three levels. The first and most important level is being called as a disciple and minister through her baptism. Francine is called by God. Simple. On a second level, Francine has received the authorization from the diocesan bishop to provide a certain type of ministry. His authorization is a letter of recommendation to the people of the diocese:

> It tells the people I am competent, credible, and entrusted with a sacred responsibility. That's in the initial stages of my ministry. Then I have to live up to that recommendation. The final level of authorization comes from the community itself. If they find in me someone who is competent, credible and trustworthy in the way I carry out a sacred responsibility, the people will respond by their trust and acceptance of me.

*

When invitations to preach in Anglican and Protestant pulpits became a regular occurrence, I was acutely aware of the importance of proper "authorization" on various levels. In this case, the congregation exercised its authority by inviting me into the pulpit. My inner authority was activated as I accepted the invitation, committing myself to prepare and deliver the sermon to the best of my ability. But I also felt the need for my own bishop's authorization. After all, even though the invitation to preach came to me personally, I and the inviting church were very aware of my Catholic constituency. So I met with my bishop to discuss these opportunities to preach and how best to handle them. We spoke of the importance of ecumenism and how my contribution to Christian unity could be most fruitful in preaching. Finally, he gave his support and blessed my ministry in prayer.

*** WYLMA and DARLENE ***

My long visit with Wylma and Darlene finally leads me to the question of authority. "What gives you joy, hope and courage?" I ask. Their response in unison evokes hearty laughter. "It is the strong conviction that we are *finally* living out our vocation," Darlene says. For her, the inner call, the acceptance of the people, and the formal mandate all need to work together to authenticate and authorize her ministry.

> Without my own sense of being called and sent by God into this ministry, any formal authorization would be a hollow formality. Without the acceptance of the people, the authorization of the bishop would be of little help. Without the bishop's authorization, I could still minister to God's people, but not formally in the name of the Church.
>
> So the answer to the question "By what authority?" is first of all that I am answering God's call. That call is recognized by the people, and is given formal authorization by the bishop.

Wylma thinks long and hard before she replies. "It is hard to explain," she says, "but there is an air of contentment in my life that I have never felt before. That in itself is what I draw on and what makes my ministry here so very much a part of my life." Wylma's reflection about what authorizes her ministry, and how the three sources of authority are interconnected, is a prime example of what this process looks like in a concrete ministry. She tells me to get comfortable as she begins to share her lengthy reply born from concrete experiences. While Wylma offers her thoughts, Darlene refills our teacups and nods in agreement.

> My view of the relationship of the various sources of authority flows from my personal history of ministry to First Nations people. First of all, my own inner authority is primary, essential, core and foundational – without it, the other dimensions of authority would be ineffective. By my own inner authority, I mean that God speaks to me in many ways, internal and external, all of which are brought to a particular focus showing God's will for me. The Spirit of God within me confirms this focus by gifts of clarity and peace and a sense of possibility and rightness.

Wylma checks to make sure I'm following her before she continues.

> The authority of the local faith community, the community I serve, is also essential. It is often implicit, with thank you's or expressions of appreciation, or it is explicit, consisting of statements confirming that Darlene and I are in the right place in terms of ministry. Among numerous remarks to this effect, one from an elder stands out: "You are the best missionaries we have ever had, because you don't push."

Knowing how deep the divide can be between white people and First Nations, I know that such a comment is not made lightly. My appreciation for my friends deepens. She adds,

> Other comments have strongly confirmed our belonging among the people. At times the authority from the faith community has been formalized; for example, in the connection with the First Nations community I presently serve. This began when the chief requested pastoral care and the bishop sent me along with Darlene. We were fully accepted from the moment we went there. After five years our formal assignment ended. Nevertheless we stayed connected to the community.

At this point in her story, I ask what it is like to do ministry without a formal mandate. "Very difficult," Wylma replies. She resumes her story.

Recently the same chief was elected again, and he explicitly requested that Darlene and I, and a third missionary who joined us this year, be sent to this Cree community again. Our bishop responded with a formal mandate. If a local faith community were to totally withdraw its authority, directly or indirectly asking us to leave, then we would see that as a clear indication to move on.

I am intrigued. These women have developed the skill of a profound listening to the people they serve, and to take their cues from them. I am not only intrigued, I am genuinely impressed. I feel like I'm sitting at their feet, learning how to listen better.

The institutional, formal authority of the Church seems to be required, at least initially. It certainly makes a difference. However, if I found only the first two dimensions of authority present, I would still feel that I could follow my call to ministry *except* in those areas that *explicitly* require the permission of the local ordinary or of the pastor of a parish, such as performing baptisms and weddings.

Wylma and Darlene's caution and respect regarding church regulations are attitudes that I both admire and support. I listen closely to Wylma's words.

We began this ministry over 20 years ago, when Darlene and I both belonged to a religious order, which we have since left. At that time, our religious order *sent* us (two women) into ministry, even though religious in some orders, including ours, were not being sent anymore. For the most part, they discerned their particular work or ministry and informed their superiors (this was a transition time from "blind obedience" to more collegial forms of discernment). The initial sending contributed to our inner discernment and sense of rightness in taking this step.

Lest I start thinking that their experience has been without bumps, Darlene talks extensively of the ambivalence that called their authority into question. For several months, their religious superiors were not sure about whether to follow through on their initial decision.

After the first three years of ministry in this location, our religious superiors became ambivalent once again while we and our pastor considered it right and necessary that we stay on that reserve. At the five-year mark, we ourselves discerned that it was time to move on. Our superiors concurred, saying, "We know it is time for you to leave, because you are not fighting to stay anymore."

Wylma explains to me the ecclesiastical geography of where their ministry took place and the differences between the two bishops.

> Interestingly, the bishop of the diocese in which we served (on the edge of the diocese) had barely a marginal interest in our presence and ministry, although together with our pastor (who lived 70 kilometres away, in the next diocese) we were instrumental in the building of a new church on the reserve. The bishop of the neighbouring diocese (our pastor's bishop), however, was highly supportive, assisted us when thorny issues required discernment, and invited us to all his pastoral development days. Much of our pastoral training came from his thoughtfulness and generosity in including us in this way.

I become aware that Wylma's understanding of how the community's authority validates her vocation has developed for over more than 20 years of ministry. I keep listening and learning.

> Our next confirmation by formal authority came when our present bishop invited us into his diocese and assigned us to Native ministry in an urban area, on a reserve and to any Aboriginal people in the region who were not otherwise served by a parish. After five years, a long period of intermittent episcopal ambivalence followed. Although we were no longer formally employed by the Church, and had left our religious order, our bishop never fully withdrew his authority from our ministry either.

Darlene admits that this episcopal ambivalence created a spiritual drag on their lives and ministry. It also caused considerable damage in the way the larger faith community perceived them, seriously limiting the strength and vitality of their ministry. I look puzzled and pained. "It is hard to explain or understand," she says, "but the issue seemed to have no forum for resolution. Now, 16 years later, our bishop has recently renewed our mandate even though we are not employed nor seeking to be employed by the diocese."

I am learning from Wylma and Darlene's experience with authority that inside call and authority need to be corroborated by the external counterpart in the Church. In the two major ministry / mission assignments that Wylma recalls, the sending authority in each instance (the religious order and the bishop) began wholeheartedly, but was followed by subsequent periods of ambivalence. In addition, in Wylma's current location, both the local faith community ("of the dominant culture – not the faith community we serve, but the faith community in whose midst we live and worship") and the clergy were often indifferent to the ministry the two women exercised in their midst. Nevertheless, throughout these years, regardless of the vitality, or lack thereof, of formal authority, Wylma reports, "Our inner authority persisted and was absolutely essential. To an extent the inner authority included the active living memory of those times when the formal authority had been very real and alive."

Currently, Wylma and Darlene are enjoying a renewal of their mandate, which was recently given by the local bishop. They both admit that this has injected new energy into their ministry.

> It feels as if a weight has been lifted, and a drag has been removed. The explicit mandate has given me a greater sense of wholeness as a person and in my relationship to the Church.

I am impressed with Wylma and Darlene's clear articulation. Their thoughtful reflection communicates that they have sincerely wrestled with and listened to the three sources of authority: within themselves, with regard to the institutional Church and in the faith community. I take their example as an inspiration for my own ongoing journey in ministry by striving at all times to work with the appropriate ecclesiastical authorities rather than against them or by doing my own thing.

*** CARLA'S EXPERIENCE ***

As Wylma and Darlene experienced intermittently, when institutional mandate is not forthcoming, ministry can be a disheartening experience. Carla has had more than her share of this situation. Before her current position as pastoral associate, she served as pastoral leader of a university parish. She was frequently discouraged when institutional affirmation was slow and hesitant.

Carla had to propose, compose and arrange for her own rite of commissioning at the start of her ministry. She was excluded from pastoral gatherings at the diocesan level. She had to initiate ministry reviews with the bishop who was supposed to oversee her work; she even tried to set up systems of accountability for lay ministers.

Despite doing all the groundwork and receiving approval for the evaluation committee, it was never utilized, and in nine years of ministry, Carla never had a proper performance review. The pastor with whom she had the most regular contact seemed unable to give or receive constructive feedback.

However, when Carla stopped expecting institutional recognition as her primary source of affirmation, her ministry began to flourish. She became more realistic in her relationship with the institutional aspect of the Church. In the most basic aspects of its management (finances, personnel, accountability structures), the institution Carla experienced was incompetent, unprofessional and driven by clerical politics from which she was excluded.

On the bright side, this exclusion provided Carla with a buffer of sorts. "I have benefited most when I have been able to keep my focus on my ministry and on the people whom I serve," she says.

*

Painful and awkward situations arise when any of the three sources of authority conflict or fail to affirm one another. When I was approached once by individuals from several parishes who wanted me to offer basic training in how to prepare and deliver homiletic reflections, I designed a simple training outline for preaching and presented it to the priests of all the parishes in the region. I informed them that the request for this type of training had come from the community, and that I wished to respond to the need. I asked for their feedback, input and approval.

My request, coming from a lay person treading in an area of ministry that was so intimately connected with priestly ministry, triggered suspicion, insecurity and fear. My transparent and respectful approach seemed to do little to alleviate personal insecurities in the clergy, and consequently no action was taken. Lay people continued to share homiletic reflections in Sunday celebrations of the Word without having access to appropriate guidance, resources and training.

There are times when I rely more on my inner authority and on the authority of the recipients of my ministry than I do on the institutional, formal authority of the Church. I believe the Church belongs to the people of God, and that as ministers we are called to serve, not be served.

> You know that the rulers of the Gentiles lord it over them, and their great ones are tyrants over them. It will not be so among you. Whoever wishes to be great among you must be your servant, and whoever wishes to be first among you must be your slave; just as the Son of Man came not to be served but to serve, and to give his life a ransom for many. (Matthew 20:25-28)

5

Sacraments and Sacramentality

And the Word became flesh and lived among us,
  and we have seen his glory,
  the glory as of a father's only son,
  full of grace and truth.

(John 1:14)

My Catholic spirit shrieked the first time I walked into the chapel at the Lutheran seminary where I was a student. Its architecture was striking in its starkness – no hint of playfulness or mystery, of devotion or imagination. Every possibility to engage the senses had been carefully circumvented. The pulpit, with its soft waves carved in the wood, was the only item that betrayed an artist's touch. The rest was brick and mortar, with a large empty cross as stark as its surroundings. Every attempt to avoid stimulating the senses and the imagination reinforced the difference between Protestant and Catholic traditions. I felt my Catholicity through what I missed: the art, the symbols, the images, the colours, the invitation to mystery. Being Catholic means being sacramental, which includes the way we furnish and decorate our worship space, because we believe that everything is a vehicle for communicating God's grace.

After a few months, once I felt a solid rapport with one of my Lutheran professors, I mentioned my negative reaction to the chapel design and furnishing. Coupled with this reaction came the question that had plagued my mind: "What happened to sacraments, and to the sacramental imagination, in your tradition?"

My professor smiled, and with a tone of both contrition and challenge, he replied, "Well, I guess we've both erred in that domain. We've perceived the Catholic sacramental system and its generous church art as bordering on magic, whereas in our Protestant zeal to differentiate ourselves from Rome, we've strayed from the meaning and power of sacraments and have trivialized them instead, along with the artistic expression, to the point of ridicule. Both our traditions have some serious work to do in reclaiming the essence, health and beauty of the sacramental life as the legacy of our Lord Jesus Christ."

Armed with that challenge, I vowed to delve more deeply into the meaning and practice of the sacramental life. A Catholic priest who was a professor in another college offered to be my adviser for an elective course. When we surveyed the sound theological, scriptural and pastoral formation I was receiving among the Lutherans, we both agreed that what was missing was the sacramental component. "To round out your comprehensive ministry formation, we need to delve into the greatest gift of Catholicism, and that is the sacraments: their history, theology and practice," he said. By now I had been a Catholic student among the Lutherans for a few years. That was enough time to become aware of some significant cultural and theological differences. The Catholic value given to the sacramental life reflects a deep theological and anthropological appreciation of the goodness of the created order, and the capacity of the material world to communicate God's grace. Lutherans focus more on original sin than on original blessing. From this perspective flows a more restrictive view of the material world's ability to act as a channel of God's grace.

So began my rediscovery of the sacramental beauty in my Catholic backyard. Under the mentorship of the Catholic priest and professor, and with the help of Joseph Martos's seminal work *Doors to the Sacred*,[12] I journeyed through the history and theology of every Catholic sacrament.

But what, in fact, is a sacrament?

*** DEANNA'S QUESTION ***

Deanna encountered this question, albeit in a different form. Her ministry experience provided part of the answer:

> The prohibition on my administering the sacraments of the Church no longer bothers me. Instead, my experience of sacrament has deepened and broadened, breaking open a confined and limited understanding of sacrament. For example, I do Fifth Steps with people in AA.[13] In the eyes of the Church, this is not considered a sacrament, but in my experience of God, of communion with the person, and of the healing power of confession, these times are profound sacramental encounters both for me and for the one doing the Fifth Step.

*

A sacrament is a door to the sacred, says Joseph Martos. The material world is capable of connecting us to God. God's primary revelation, therefore, or God's primordial sacrament, is all of creation, that vast, breathtaking arena of nature where the human–divine encounter awaits us, surprises us, overwhelms us. Nature is imbued with God's divine light, the same light that shines from our own inner beings and is revealed through our eyes. This light might be most noticeable when it is absent. I have seen children whose eyes have already grown dim as a result of enormous suffering in their young lives. I have looked over the lake on a dull, grey day and felt as if nature itself was mourning.

God's light animates our demeanour and our engagement with the world. I can tell by looking into someone's eyes if the divine light is allowed to shine freely, or if it has been covered over by pain and struggle. The task of ministry is to seek the light in another, and to set it free. This is profound sacramental work, the work of making God's inward grace visible on the outside.

What creates profound sadness in me is the notion that some of our primary sacramental celebrations in the Church seem to betray an undervaluing of this holy work in ministry. In some ways it is almost "better" not to know too much of what could be. For example, since my initial firsthand experience of God's healing touch in sacramental confession during an encounter that was not restricted by time, and was facilitated by a confessor who entered into meaningful conversation, I have had great difficulty with the mechanical approach to the sacrament of reconciliation. I wonder if the lineups at confession time, which force the briefest exchange with the priest, result in a mere skimming of the surface on issues and sins that often require much more attention and care. Swept up by the power of immersion baptism of an adult at the Easter Vigil, I now cringe at what looks to me as a minimalist approach to baptism: how does the standard use of a few drops of water for baptism fully reflect the dramatic dying and rising with Christ that baptism signifies? After I have tasted Eucharistic celebrations where great care was taken for good liturgy – in song, presiding, prayer and decor – without time restrictions, half-hour Masses that reduce participating to mechanical responses feel like a betrayal of the power of both liturgy and sacrament. How can we taste the richness of God's banquet in these moments?

I once attended a Saturday evening Mass that included a baptism. The priest was squeezed for time as he had to hurry to another parish. He cut corners wherever he could in both the baptismal rite and the Eucharistic celebration. He rushed through the prayers, sounding more like an auctioneer than a minister of the Gospel facilitating a sacred encounter. The sprinkling of a few drops of water barely resembled immersion into the death of the Lord and rising into his resurrection. I sorely missed the careful attention and the human warmth that this young family deserved. My heart sank, aching for the young parents of the child being baptized, for the assembly of the faithful, and for the whole Church. What kind of human–divine encounter was being facilitated here?

My professor's reply echoed in my ears: we Catholics have been, and continue to be, guilty of both trivializing and minimizing the sacramental encounter, and of treating sacraments as magic. I sighed.

*** LENORA'S MINISTRY ***

Diminished celebrations of the sacraments deprive us of opportunities to taste their potential power. This often leads to a reduction of sacramental preoccupations, focusing primarily on external details and mechanical involvements. As a woman in ministry, Lenora has looked deeply into the core meaning of sacramentality. She sees the Church hung up on rubrics rather than concerned about facilitating a sacramental encounter.

> If I could administer the sacrament of reconciliation, my ministry of pastoral counselling with young university students would be even more effective, particularly for women and people who say they won't talk with a priest about certain issues. Regarding the celebration of the Eucharist, the prohibition affects my ministry differently depending on the priests with whom I am working. One priest can be a good partner, respectful of everyone and open to positive communication. The style of another priest can sometimes alienate people from the community, which makes my job harder.

Initially, Lenora was given an ecclesiastical mandate to provide baptisms, weddings and funerals for Catholics in the university community. This mandate was empowering, but somewhat intimidating at first. Even though her Master of Divinity formation had included lots of training in liturgical celebration, she had never imagined that she herself would serve in that way. "I have found baptisms to be a great way of introducing families to the parish," she says. "Before this mandate, for pastoral reasons, I would facilitate the family's connection with the baptismal preparation program in the nearby parish and rarely provided one on campus."

As Lenora grew more comfortable in a presiding role, she appreciated being able to preside at weddings and to demonstrate that the Church was changing, especially when she was ministering to people on campus, many of whom had concerns about gender issues in the Church. On these occasions, Lenora frequently received feedback that people, especially young people on campus, felt more interested in the Church when they learned that its ministry was becoming more open to women. Somehow young people saw in Lenora a role model who stood close to their own lives by virtue of being female and non-ordained. For some, these occasions led to active participation in the Catholic Church again. Some even became involved in ministry themselves.

*** AUDREY'S STRUGGLE ***

Ministering in a non-ordained capacity in a sacramental church, however, creates a painful crucible. In her work as hospital chaplain, Audrey struggles with the separation between pastoral and sacramental ministry. She walks with people in times of illness, death, recovery. She is called to pray with them, to help them find hope and to discover God in their suffering. Audrey leads prayer services in the hospital chapel. She has done simple funeral prayers and performs the occasional baptism.

Many of these times are truly holy encounters for her. But when the sacrament of the sick is requested, Audrey must call a priest. Roman Catholic teaching upholds the privilege of an ordained priest to administer this sacrament. This limitation on her ministry raises multiple questions and creates a unique kind of pain.

> Often the priest does not know the people. He comes in, does the ritual (anointing, and sometimes confession) and leaves. I am allowed to journey with people before and after the sacraments.

> This separation of the pastoral from the sacramental ministry fractures the necessary unity between the two. It is not good for the priest or for me in my role as chaplain. And it hurts to have to call a priest to do something that I feel called to do as part of my ministry.

*** GLADYS'S PAIN ***

Gladys shares Audrey's pain. She believes that she is Christ's presence in the world, and that she is called to be about the building up of God's reign on this earth. Gladys preaches the Gospel – sometimes at church – and often as she prepares couples and individuals for the sacraments.

With some reluctance and regret in her voice, Gladys explains:

> I am a "pastor," and feel I shepherd our people in ways that many of our priests do not or choose not to do. I often will make the extra call, take someone out to lunch who is struggling, enquire about how a family member is doing after losing a loved one.

She does not want to "pick on" priests, but her experience gives her the impression that some priests regard their ministry primarily through rubrics and rules. In a previous job in hospital chaplaincy, she had the repeated experiences of the priest refusing to visit a sick person in the hospital, because he "had already done his thing" – that is, he had anointed the person. His job was done, whereas Gladys often felt that her job was just beginning. It was Gladys who continued to be available for significant encounters with the patient and his or her loved ones, helping them cope with the reality of illness or imminent death.

> When I was in hospital chaplaincy, and now in parish work, I lament that I cannot give the sacrament of the sick. Especially here in the north, good Catholics die without receiving the sacrament because the priest is too far away. I would also like to be able to baptize those whom I prepare, as well as officiate at marriages, as I am the one involved with the people right up to the celebration of the sacraments.

*** DEANNA'S REPLY ***

The pain expressed by Audrey and Gladys is real. It ought not to be played down. When we focus on the deeper primary function and meaning of a sacrament, however, limited "churchy" notions can break wide open. When that happens women in ministry realize, often to their own surprise, that their work is profoundly sacramental.

"Do I hear confessions in jail? All the time, lots!" Deanna tells me.

> One time an inmate did an AA Fifth Step with me. I listened for several hours as he poured out all the pain from years of violence, abuse and neglect. As I listened to his broken heart, I felt like Jesus taking on our burdens and our pain. I offered him God's love and assured him of God's forgiveness.

> At the end he asked for absolution. I had to tell him that I couldn't give him that because I was not ordained, but that I would arrange for him to see a priest. Several days later, the inmate met with the priest. He was in and out in ten minutes. When I saw the peace on his face as he walked out of the room, I knew in an instant what had happened: his "real" confession had been in the

hours spent with me. Seeing the priest fulfilled his need for the Church's ritual. So, tell me, in this case, what is sacrament and when exactly did it occur?

Deanna hastens to add that she considers ordained priesthood important – very important, even. In fact, her ministry experience has helped her understand the significance and the necessity of priestly ministry. The priest does act as a mediator between the person and God, and becomes a visible sign of God's invisible presence and action. Human beings need this sacramental presence in the person who is duly called and consecrated to fulfill this role. However, she has serious reservations about how she sees the priesthood lived and defined today. Something is not quite right, she says. There is, for Deanna, too much magic attributed to the priesthood, reinforced by the Church's talk of special "powers." Priests behave and speak in ways that reinforce their separateness from, and sometimes their perceived superiority over, the laity rather than their commonality as baptized members of Christ's body. Deanna has been challenged by inmates who question her about the difference between a magician and a priest, and this only adds to her concern. Deanna doesn't think priesthood was originally meant that way. As I listen to her, I hear once again echoes of my professor's words: "We've perceived the Catholic sacramental system and its generous church art as bordering on magic."

Deanna's own ministry is helping her correct such misperceptions. She explains,

> I've come to understand sacrament as sacred presence, a touch of the divine, and that has liberated me. For example, I work together with a female Protestant minister. She celebrates Eucharist with the inmates and they have a deep encounter with Jesus in the bread and the wine. Who am I to say this is not "correct"?

*** WYLMA'S and GLADYS'S PEOPLE ***

According to Gladys, First Nations people are naturally sacramental. They experience the sacredness of the Creator through all material signs. However, she adds that access to the sacraments of the Church is more difficult for them than for many other members of the Church.

Behind these difficulties lie the effects of prejudice in the dominant society (including the church "establishment"), and the Church's lack of adaptation and cultural sensitivity in the requirements of sacramental preparation. Wylma concurs, adding that First Nations people experience a general lack of welcome and acceptance (for example, at Sunday Eucharistic celebrations) that could be expressed in culturally suitable ways. The sacrament of reconciliation is virtually inaccessible to rural Native or reserve communities. "I find that my ministry includes teaching people the many ways that God forgives us, that we need only turn to God with sorrow for sin and that God forgives us," she says.

Wylma and Gladys are allowed to celebrate baptisms under certain conditions, such as in Native communities where no priest is available. Both point out that in many places and for long periods of time, however, the people have been largely deprived of all sacraments. Says Wylma, "At times even priests who were technically 'available' for the reserve to which I ministered, in fact did not go to the reserve for which they had pastoral responsibility, or went very infrequently."

*** CARLA'S ANOINTING ***

A deep sacramental awareness and appreciation not only expands limited categories and definitions, and not only enriches the experience of lay ministry, it also opens us to sacramental affirmations of our call and our ministry.

Carla experienced this in a very potent way. Her sense of a vocation or call to serve the Church as a lay ecclesial minister has evolved naturally over time. As in all vocations, Carla describes the onset as a honeymoon phase, a time when the signs were very clear, even in a sacramental sense. Carla recalls an experience during a Chrism Mass early on in her ministry.

> I was asked by the pastor to prepare the cruets of Holy Oils for our parish representatives to take to the liturgy. I forgot to do it until later in the day of the Chrism Mass. In emptying the cruets of oil into the receptacle (the old oil was to be burned during the Easter Vigil), I accidentally spilled the Sacred

Chrism on my hands because I was in such a rush. I nevertheless got the cruets ready on time. I then debated whether I would actually attend the Chrism Mass, as it is a liturgy where the focus on ordained ministry is sometimes painfully exclusive of the other forms of ministry within the Church. I finally decided to go.

I am curious about what will follow, and listen attentively.

The homily was indeed focused exclusively on ordained ministry. I felt excluded and didn't want to listen. But then something happened. The bishop focused a great deal on how the Sacred Chrism was used to anoint the priest's hands during the liturgy of ordination, and how this symbolic action consecrates the ordained minister for service. All at once I could smell something. I sought out the source of the fragrance and realized that I was the one with the Sacred Chrism on my hands that night. I had been "ordained" or affirmed in my vocation through my own service!

I smiled, for I could not help thinking: was this an "accident" of the Holy Spirit?

*** SHARON'S APPRECIATION ***

In her work of preparing children and adults for the sacraments of initiation, Sharon has been growing in her understanding and experience of the sacraments. While she has always found them to be a beautiful aspect of the Church, she now has a much deeper appreciation for how they are celebrated and what they mean. It is so easy, Sharon says, for persons born into the Catholic Church to take the sacramental life for granted.

Now in charge of all sacramental preparations, as well as RCIA, Sharon has come to view the sacraments in a whole new light where their beauty and spirituality shine.

Sacraments facilitate an encounter with Christ Jesus and with one another as the Body of Christ. The sacramental experience in my life and the experience of sacraments in the Church allow me to grow in my call to be an example and role model.

Sacraments – in particular the Eucharist – are intimate encounters with God, almost a kind of love-making. A kind of mystical experience is made possible through the sacramental encounter. For me, the sacrament of reconciliation has become the primary place of healing, of purging and of peace.

For Sharon, who has served as parish pastoral leader for nearly nine years now, sacraments and liturgy have taken on a completely new meaning. As a parish minister, she is visibly the leader of the community, but she cannot preside at Mass. Her presence in the sanctuary is a paradox: "Before I was a parish minister, my worship was somewhat communal and somewhat personal. Since I have become the parish minister, I find that it is more exclusively communal."

She considers it important to be positioned in the sanctuary during Mass as well as in lay services. The community she currently serves has had a sequence of short, unhappy placements with pastors, during which Sharon's constancy has been a reassuring sign of permanent leadership.

"I know that not all parish ministers stay in the sanctuary during the liturgy, but I believe it is very important. It also has validated my appointment by the bishop to be here," she tells me. Her identity as leader is very much tied to the liturgy, because that is when most parishioners see her. However, the celebration of the sacraments exacerbates her alienation from the hierarchy and the institution.

"What do you mean by that?" I ask. Sharon explains that she spends a lot of time with all sorts of people in preparation for the sacraments, in teaching about them, in sharing her own belief and the Church's teaching about them, but she is not allowed to bestow the actual sacraments themselves. This prohibition is a regular source of sorrow, pain and frustration.

*

When sacraments are celebrated with their appropriate fullness of meaning, they become powerful vehicles of God's communication. In and through the sacraments I am touched and fed far beyond the external ritual. When this happens, I move from an objective action that occurs largely outside of me and is "done to me," to a transforming encounter inside of me.

I recall Eucharistic celebrations where this holy encounter was tangible and profound. Often, these have been intimate and informal celebrations in which the participation of each person present was valued. They have also occurred in large celebrations where great care was given to liturgical richness and beauty to engage all the senses.

For the sake of our own Catholic integrity, and for the sake of Christian unity, we would do well to heed the importance of our sacramental tradition. Of all the Christian traditions, the Catholic one is the custodian of the sacramental door that leads us to an encounter with the sacred. This increases our responsibility to be worthy keepers of the treasure so we can share it with the world. The pain experienced by many Christians over the fact that the Eucharistic table continues to be a source of division ought to increase our responsibility for taking our own sacramental practices more seriously.

*** DEANNA'S ILLUSTRATION ***

Deanna, reflecting on prison culture, has a candid way of illustrating this point.

> When we throw out the sacred, the violence within ourselves and in society at large increases. I see this in the lives of the inmates. Once an inmate re-establishes a connection with the sacred, he can start rebuilding his life; he can start looking at himself, warts and all. And they have a blunt way of showing when the Sacred, God, starts hounding them.

> Initially they don't like it, because it's not cool to get religion. They resist, yet God's love pulls them – in different ways at different times for different guys. But when it happens, it's unmistakable. I simply walk with them as they attempt to reconnect their lives with the sacred first of all within themselves. From this initial connection grows their ability to reconnect with the sacred outside of themselves and take control of their violent behaviour.

*** GLADYS'S BAPTISM ***

Gladys adds a sacramental flavour from her ministry experience.

I accompanied a pregnant parishioner to the hospital. Her baby was born prematurely. All indications pointed to the baby's early death. The woman wanted her baby boy baptized; we couldn't find a priest anywhere near this isolated community. We invited the nurse to join us. I lit a candle and prepared a small bowl of water. We shared spontaneous prayers, I read Luke 3:21-22 from my pocket Bible, and I baptized that baby "in the name of the Father, and of the Son, and of the Holy Spirit." The words from Scripture washed over the tiny baby and his young mother: "This is my beloved son, in whom I am well pleased." It was a profound sacramental experience. Several hours later, the baby died.

*

Vatican II theology supports the understanding that, in the authentic experience of sacrament, the "sacramental power" of the ordained is shared with the faithful. This sharing in turn activates the priestly aspect of the faithful themselves, thereby offering sacrifice together with the ordained presbyter. As my own bishop summarized in a talk on the Eucharist, the sacramental action of the assembly is the offering of their own lives in sacrifice, grafted onto the sacrifice of Christ on the cross. In its fullest expression, Eucharist gathers us to give praise and thanks, to offer ourselves with Christ in sacrifice, to become a people of communion without limits, and to be sent forth to bring Good News.

Far from being an object to observe and adore, Eucharist is a verb, a dynamic action of taking, blessing, breaking and sharing the Body and Blood of our Lord and, by inference, the lives of each person partaking. By trivializing, minimizing or focusing primarily on the external reality of Eucharist, we miss the essential transforming nature and purpose of Eucharist. All sacraments carry such a transforming purpose.

*** MARLENE'S FOCUS ***

Even though it is not easy, Marlene has learned to look beyond the trivial aspects of sacramental celebrations, beyond the exclusive practices in the Church, while still focusing on the body of Christ. Eucharist has great meaning for her because it is about Christ and his power to transform, not about the institutional Church. As a Catholic, Marlene loves the rich sacramental traditions, and they are part of who she is. In an attempt to hide her own pain, however, she often finds herself saying to strangers, when asked what she does,

> I work for a non-profit Catholic organization that seeks to proclaim the Good News in innovative ways.... I guess I look at the theology of sacraments and sometimes feel the need to distance myself from the way they are practised. The theology is beautiful; the practice sometimes is stifling.

*

The sacramental connection between the visible and the invisible is an intriguing one. It is possible for women in ministry to experience a sacramental dimension to their divine calling without having that calling "made visible" through the sacramental sign of Holy Orders. Sacramental theology of Vatican II defines a sacrament as a visible sign in the communal celebration of the people of God, united in Christ Jesus, of an invisible experience or reality of grace. The Church's celebration of the sacrament makes visible a reality that already exists.

This understanding has helped me name my experience of call into pastoral ministry. For all intents and purposes, I may well live an "ordained" ministerial reality without the outward – visible – sign of the sacrament of Holy Orders. This has both liberating and stifling effects. Liberating, since I know deep in my heart the mark of God's priestly "ordaining" activity which is confirmed by the *fiat* of the faith community I serve. Stifling, because, while withholding the sacrament of orders, the Church is at the same time ignoring the need to create other legitimate structural blessings that mandate the pastoral leadership exercised by women. Not only is this need for the proper ordering of non-ordained ministries ignored, there has been a formal closing of the discussion on the ordination of women. This means that there is, as yet, no ecclesiastical willingness to recognize the reality that I, and possibly many others, already live as a woman called by God to serve in ecclesial ministry.

***LIVING A SACRAMENTAL MINISTRY ***

Nearly all the women with whom I spoke for the purposes of this book readily admitted the sacramental conundrum they find themselves in. Carla ponders this reality.

> I prepare liturgies, attend liturgies, teach about liturgy, preach at liturgies, but am prohibited, by gender, from celebrating the first and foremost liturgy – the Eucharist. It used to bother me, and at some level the injustice of it still does, but as I have grown more into who and what God wants me to be, I feel that I am doing what I am meant to be doing. Would I now want to take that step to ordination if it was possible? I cannot say for sure.

People often tell Sharon that, since she prepares them for the sacraments, it doesn't seem right that she cannot preside over the administration of the sacraments. The one reason Sharon would want to be able to administer the sacraments is to bring to fulfillment the sacredness that she shares with people on the journey of preparation. Being present at the ceremony as a "spectator," where the priest who presides does not know the people and just "flew" in for the ceremony, is not quite the same.

*

My own pastoral experience has not involved preparing parishioners for sacraments. I find myself more involved in the preaching of the Word. I call it preaching, even though when a woman or another lay person engages in deliberate study and speaking on the Scriptures, it is called a reflection. Whenever I "preach" in talks at retreats or workshops, people tell me they are touched. This type of affirmation has helped me to grow as a minister in the Church. When others deem my offering worthwhile, I am encouraged to trust, to grow and to dare in other areas, too.

The challenge is to let God guide me, because there are still times when my ego wants to take over. When I allow God to lead, I can trust that my "preaching" will contain words that need to be said, rather than what I want to say. This is deep sacramental work.

*** FRANCINE'S SELF-IDENTITY ***

Working in diocesan ministry, Francine does not assist people in preparing for the sacraments either, so they are not a direct part of her ministry as such. Some sacraments, however, have a strong relationship to Francine's self-identity.

> Baptism and confirmation are key sacraments because of what they signify in terms of being grafted onto Christ, plunged into the paschal mystery and being empowered by the Spirit. Books have been written on this topic – it's too big to do it justice in a few words. Eucharist is central. What comes to mind here is becoming Eucharist for the life of the world.
>
> That is a mystery that I try to spend time on. How does my life become a reflection of the life of Christ? How does my life give honour, praise and glory to God and witness to the life that God offers? If I were to name a sacrament that has had the most impact on me, I would name the sacrament of reconciliation – especially in conjunction with good spiritual direction. For years I avoided the sacrament because of bad past experiences, inordinate guilt, not wanting to face certain questions, etc. Over the past several years I have come to a very new place in my understanding and experience of this sacrament and the value of spiritual direction in ministry.

With all the exciting new forms of ministry in which we find ourselves as non-ordained Catholic women, there is, however, an increasing realization of the intrinsic connection between the ministry of Word, of sacramental ministry, and of pastoral leadership. To exercise pastoral ministry disconnected from sacramental ministry feels fragmented. This fragmentation can be the cause of deep personal pain, especially if one feels called to do all three. Fragmentation can occur whenever any of these three integral aspects of the call to ministry is severed from the other two. I experienced this most poignantly in a recent preaching experience.

I was invited to be a guest preacher for a Sunday service of the Word. Scanning the lectionary readings, I was drawn by the first reading from Genesis with particular intensity. Even in ideal circumstances, it was not an easy text – the account of Abraham's sacrifice of Isaac. But this particular Sunday came in the aftermath of a terrible traffic accident in a community where three sixteen-year-olds were killed and three other teenagers remained in hospital in critical condition. What made the Abraham and Isaac account even more potent was the fact that one family had lost their only child in this tragedy, while another bereaved family were members of the parish in which I was to preach.

The Sunday of my preaching followed the week in which the funerals of the three teenagers took place. So here I was, a guest preacher from outside, having had no pastoral contact with any of the people affected so deeply by this sorrowful event. I had not attended any of the funerals, and now I was to be preaching on a text that spoke of child sacrifice! I was sweating, and not just a little. On the one hand, I could not ignore what had occurred in that community and what was surely on the minds of those in church that Sunday morning. On the other hand, how could I weave together the themes of the Genesis lesson and my preaching with this tragedy when I lacked any personal pastoral connection to the events surrounding the accident and the individuals affected by it?

I took some risks and dared to name the tragedy in connection with Abraham's sacrifice of Isaac. I prayed that the words I offered that morning would help people make sense of what had occurred in their midst. The parents who had lost their daughter were absent that morning, but another parishioner asked for the text of my sermon, adding, "I want to take these words to [the parents], for they need this right now." I breathed a sigh of relief mixed with deep gratitude. However, I felt acutely the disadvantage of having my preaching disconnected from the pastoral role of ministry, just as I had so often felt pain over the lack of connection between my pastoral involvement with people and the Church's sacramental ministry.

*** GLADYS'S FRAGMENTATION ***

Gladys concurs with my feelings of fragmentation. She is acutely aware of the unique position she occupies in the northern parish community as its pastoral and liturgical leader. Although deeply involved as a liturgical leader, she is nevertheless prohibited from celebrating sacraments. No matter where we find ourselves in ministry, we cannot avoid this dilemma.

> I feel extremely blessed to have the opportunity to attend weekday Mass in another community. Also, I am in the rare position of leading a communion service once a week. I conduct daily and Sunday communion services when the priest is gone (if the time were totalled, this would be about sixteen weeks of the year). I also preach the first Sunday of every month and on special feast days.

Gladys tries as much as possible to live her ministry as an integrated whole.

> I have grown to appreciate the intimate connection between liturgy and the pastoral ministry I exercise in the parish. My liturgical leadership is derived from, and flows out of, my pastoral leadership in the parish. That is why, as a pastoral minister, it is so important to have this ministry reflected in some form of leadership within the liturgy. Yet, when it comes to giving the children First Communion, I cannot do that.

*

It seems to me that there exists an ironic twist of events. Women in pastoral ministry have no sacramental mandate. Nevertheless, these same women are in fact contributing to a deeper understanding and experience of the Church's sacramental heritage. It is my heartfelt prayer that women's rich sacramental offering of self to the people of God may contribute to the entire Church's appreciation of the sacramental nature of life, ministry and worship.

6

Together in Ministry

In the image of God he created them;
male and female he created them.
(Genesis 1:27)

Long car rides on the prairies are great places for good conversation. Fr. Daniel and I were on a mission. We both knew that increasing numbers of lay people were presiding and preaching at Sunday celebrations of the Word with communion, since many parishes were being served by priests with multiple charges great distances apart. Fr. Daniel and I shared a deep passion and appreciation for good preaching. We teamed up, with one another and with the diocesan liturgy commission, to consider bringing a training course in lay preaching to several dioceses in our Prairie province. On this particular two-hour trip, we were heading to a meeting of the priests' council in a neighbouring diocese to present our case. I expressed my appreciation for the team approach, pointing out the complementary elements that our relationship modelled: lay and ordained, male and female, married and celibate, biological mother and spiritual father. Smiling, Fr. Daniel agreed. At the same time he voiced his regret that not many priests seem to feel comfortable with this type of collaboration.

Fr. Daniel's trust, enthusiasm and commitment in turn increased my own confidence and hope that we were really onto something. I believed wholeheartedly that, as a lay woman, I complemented the pastoral ministry of male clergy in many ways. Our resolve to form a team was empowering. Women offer experiences and perspectives that arise not only from being female, but also out of being fully part of the people of God, as one of the flock. As women we have sat in the pews for years. We know, through our own reflection and experience, what we need for ourselves and our families. We have learned from talking to fellow parishioners what helps nourish our faith and what stifles our spirits.

As several women in this book repeatedly illustrate, support and scorn for our ministerial presence come in a strange mix. At times, I earn surprising gratitude and respect from parishioners who may at first have been suspicious of my pastoral role. "I didn't know a woman could preside so well at a funeral vigil," one man told me.

In some church circles, I am respected for what I do and who I am as a woman in ministry; in others, I am not. Backbiting and gossip among parishioners, often driven by rivalry, jealousy or rash judgments, can obstruct effective ministry. Sometimes it is a blessing to be a fellow parishioner called into a pastoral role, because it helps both me and the other parishioners to identify with and trust one another. At other times, that same identification makes it more difficult to establish credibility and trust – a variation of the suspicion expressed toward Jesus: "Is not this the carpenter's son?" (Matthew 13:55) The ability to cope with change, the uncertainty caused by the shortage of priests, and people's level of maturity in faith development greatly affect their ability to regard a lay woman as a pastoral resource.

The same can be said of a lay woman's collaboration with clergy. When honest efforts are made to empower parishioners in their own ministerial calling, both within and outside the Church, priests and women in pastoral ministry can harness their differences for the good of the community and model a collaborative ministry style that fosters the growth and health of each. Challenges and tensions between ordained and lay pastoral staff are caused by a complex mix of personality traits and visions of ministry, faith experiences and pastoral self-identities. Some priests are very sensitive about their role as clergy and feel easily threatened. Instead of focusing on what they can fruitfully contribute to the whole, some lay women exercise their ministry with an over-emphasis on entitlement, or with too much anger and bitterness over what they are prohibited from doing.

The ensuing tensions often obstruct the realization of the genuine potential for fruitful joint ministry. These challenges are caused as much by the differences between male and female, between lay and clergy, as they are by differences in personal histories and competing visions for ministry.

*** CARLA'S FRUSTRATION ***

It continues to be my hope and prayer that negative experiences with Catholic priests are nevertheless sufficiently balanced by positive ones. Carla has had, unfortunately, mostly negative experiences. She looks pained, and a real sense of regret permeates her tone of voice. She has found it hard to develop healthy relationships with priests and do ministry together without encountering complications. Most of Carla's relationships in ministry with the ordained have not ended well.

Our conversation causes Carla to take stock. She wonders now whether her negative experiences happened because she asked for more than was possible – time, attention, energy, etc. When Carla got married, she was deeply hurt by a priest whom she considered a close friend and who subsequently shut her out of his life. "Some of my female friends said he just couldn't handle me 'belonging' to someone else. I don't know." Her voice trails off. She is lost in thought, aching to understand.

*

As Carla finishes speaking, it is my turn to be lost in thought. My mind scans the list of priests I have known. I, too, have felt the ambivalence. I, too, have experienced the artificial distance in my relationship with a priest, as if he were trying to protect himself from getting too close. And then, once, I encountered a priest who exuded a refreshing integrity and entertained a friendship. I realized how much I had longed to be able to be "just friends" with a priest.

Our initial encounters were a bit rocky; misunderstandings galore created distance and put a halt to our communications. Somehow we tried again the following year. This time we had both learned, and we displayed a new openness to one another. Our visits by phone and in person enriched us both; we shared our journeys of faith and ministry, we swapped notes on homilies and preaching. We enjoyed a glass of wine, laughter and good food. Unfortunately, our fragile friendship lasted only a mere three months. One day he made it abundantly clear he wanted no more contact. I still don't know what happened. Maybe I made some wrong moves. Maybe I disclosed too much, too soon. Maybe I was too demanding. I have stopped trying to second-guess and to blame myself. But suddenly the e-mails and phone calls stopped; it was over. Why is it so hard to be friends with a Catholic priest?

*** DEANNA'S VIEW ***

Sexual dynamics operate both consciously and unconsciously in all relationships, not just in male–female ones. If such dynamics are not openly acknowledged and worked with, however, they can exert an unhealthy power and influence. Deanna points out that sexual dynamics between women ministers and priests can be especially fraught with unspoken, unhealthy and unresolved dynamics. She nods in firm agreement when I suggest that this topic needs to be addressed in this book. Deanna is of the opinion that such discussion does not happen often enough, is not handled frankly enough, and is not undertaken by those who need it most and who would therefore benefit the most. Deanna explains:

> Sexuality, and how we are called into relationship with others, is something that healthy teams learn to integrate in healthy ways. They play together, pray together, and work together, while celebrating individual gifts and patterns of relating. I have known good priests who are comfortable in their own skin, and who can celebrate and affirm my giftedness as a colleague in ministry. This is not always the case, but I feel fortunate to know some of these presbyters and I count them among my friends.

I can tell from Deanna's voice that such friendships are sometimes hard-won and therefore deeply treasured.

*** ANNETTE'S BELIEFS ***

When I ask her in our phone conversations about male and female dynamics in ministry, Annette's voice betrays some hesitation. She wants so much to be able to say that such dynamics are positive. But she admits that this is not the case for her, at least not in her current situation. She begins by clarifying her belief that women and men need each other for balance and wholeness.

> The Church's own theology of sexual complementarities of men and women supports this understanding. The Gospel enjoys a fuller expression when both women and men function in ministry leadership.

She becomes reflective, first describing how important it is to her that she is present to whoever needs a listening ear – men, women or children. The particular pastor to whom Annette is the assistant is, however, a very difficult personality. "Dynamics" between them are not good. She says, "I try to be respectful of the priesthood that our pastor exercises while only speaking with him on parish business. However, our different temperaments hinder effective ministry and are a source of deep sadness and pain for me." She mourns the lost potential while cherishing the dream of what could be.

*** GLADYS'S OPINION ***

Gladys sees a real difference, in general, between the acceptance and respect given to men and to women in the Church. Women have yet, in her opinion, to receive the full respect they deserve. Her experience tells her that women's value in ministry is not fully appreciated or utilized primarily because of the dominance of male leadership in the Church. However, she found a striking difference in the level of acceptance by the people when she arrived in the North. She takes a far greater sacramental and spiritual leadership role in the North than she ever did in the "South." Throughout northern Canada, women like Gladys perform funerals, baptisms, weddings (occasionally), sacramental preparation, communion services and more.

In essence, we run the church, with the priest coming out once or twice a month to celebrate Mass. The people have accepted this and are very supportive; this proves that it can and does work to have women running things.

*** LENORA'S MIXED BLESSING ***

Lenora received her theology degree only a few years ago. It so happened that her class included several young, single women. They shared classes with seminarians and formed friendships with several of them. Together they became a vibrant community of faith, all on fire with a call from God to serve the Church. Several young men were still unsure of their calling, but no one was put down for doubts and questioning.

Nevertheless, Lenora remembers that there was a strange feeling in the air. Over time it became clear that male–female friendships, and the presence of women students, were not welcomed by all faculty and students. According to Lenora, some of the young seminarians projected their own sexual insecurity onto the women students. The young women students were viewed with suspicion, as in "What are you doing here?"

One seminarian discerned that priesthood was not his calling and left. A year later he became Lenora's husband.

> When the news of our relationship became public, I was toppled from the popularity list and basically shunned for any social or liturgical events. It was a shock to both of us that such unhealthy dynamics still operate in our Church and are even part of the process for priestly formation. And what about women's calling in the Church? Does anyone care to help us discern?

*

Hearing Lenora's experience saddened me deeply and raised troubling questions. Insights from the human sciences about psychosexual development for both heterosexual and homosexual individuals have taught us much. When the Vatican issued its document on homosexuality and the priesthood in the Fall of 2005, several Canadian bishops rightly pointed out that the demands for a healthy integration of one's sexuality apply to both heterosexual and homosexual candidates for the priesthood.[14]

Along with a broad acknowledgment of the importance of sound pastoral leadership, I had great hopes that today's seminary training would take the psychosexual integration of its students very seriously. I had expected that seminarians would display much healthier attitudes towards women. I had expected that young seminarians would be helped to grow a mature sexual identity, whether heterosexual or homosexual, which in turn would equip them to live their celibate charism fruitfully and without fearing intimate friendships. This task is even more pressing in light of the clergy sexual abuse scandals that have surfaced in many dioceses across North America and beyond.

I pressed Lenora some more. How can she be so sure that her experience wasn't the exception? Maybe, she admits. That's as far as she's ready to go. Her experience has left her hurt and discouraged about the moral and sexual maturity of new priests. "In the four years of sharing classroom space and social time with seminarians," she says, "I saw and heard very little evidence that these young men are in any way assisted in coming to terms with their own sexuality, let alone with the demands of celibacy."

I still want so much to believe that Lenora's experience was the exception rather than the rule. Maybe I am in denial, or maybe I want to give priests and seminarians the benefit of the doubt. It can't be all that bad; it just can't be. But Lenora's story and her subsequent bitter and troublesome conclusions keep bothering me. In my mind I can see Rev. Donald Cozzens, who writes on contemporary priesthood, nod his head in recognition.[15] Finally, I raise the topic with a good friend who has been a Catholic priest for many years. He doesn't sound all that surprised. He points out that if celibacy is not integrated in a mature manner, and if it is not inclusive of healthy intimate friendships, in particular with women, it can create a "third gender," especially in diocesan priests who are not members of a religious order. According to my ordained friend, our seminaries still produce celibate men who are not sufficiently challenged to grow through the relational demands so characteristic of intimate relationships. He illustrates this in very simple, practical terms.

"Most of us priests live alone in rectories and do not have to share living space with other individuals who would make unreasonable demands on us," he explains. "This insulated existence has dangerous consequences for how we exercise our ministry in the parish."

My priest friend's observation sounds discouraging. Yet his words also serve to help me understand the lonely reality of many ordained men. Not having a family to come home to, or not having to attend to other relational responsibilities, priests easily immerse themselves completely in their work, to the detriment of their own emotional and mental well-being. Encouraged by a theology that rewards self-sacrifice, priests become prime candidates for developing into workaholics and living over-stressed lives.

My friend's observation also helps me appreciate the great divide in life experience that exists between celibate ordained clergy and non-ordained women (many of whom are married) in ministry. There is no doubt in my mind that celibacy is a God-given charism with great value and witnessing power, especially in today's society. If the charism, however, is clouded by inadequate formation and unresolved intimacy issues, its power to be a sign of prophetic witness is seriously compromised. If an unhealthy sexual integration is left unchallenged, the celibate priest will struggle to live this charism with any kind of integrity.

Intimate relationships are the place where we "work out our salvation," as one author has said.[16] For me, being married to Jim for over 27 years serves that purpose. Married life keeps chipping away at the rough edges that obstruct my loving and fruitful living, forever treating me as a work in progress. In order to stay married, I have had to learn, sometimes the hard way, about the need for compromise and dialogue, for forgiveness and reconciliation, for patience and trust, for courage and perseverance. In turn, the training ground in marriage has helped to develop qualities that now serve me well in the various roles I fulfill in ministry.

Ideally, religious communities made up of professed members (who make vows of obedience, chastity and poverty) are intended to be the relational substitute for marriage. In Genesis 2:18, God acknowledges that it is not good for us to be alone. We grow through intimate relationships, either the exclusive one in marriage, or the relationships with others in our community. It seems to follow, then, that celibacy is likely lived out best in the context of a religious community. Come to think of it, the priests with whom I have the best connections are indeed members of religious orders.

*** GLADYS'S SURPRISE ***

It is understandable that the rapport women in ministry have with ordained presbyters remains a mixed bag that sometimes contains explosive material. At the same time, the community's response to our ministry remains a delightful surprise. When Gladys first arrived in the North, she was amazed at the community's acceptance of her role regarding the sacraments and communion services. Having lived just over 40 years in the more populated south of Canada, where women struggled to be accepted in the role of spiritual leaders or to have much of a say in the parish, Gladys observes,

> Here in the North, people turn to whoever is available at that time – either the priest or me. Very little distinction is made between us. I would find it very difficult to go back and work in a parish where the acceptance is not so great. If only the powers that be could have the same respect for and acceptance of women working in the Church and running a parish – how much better we would all be! I feel the benefits would be enormous.

*** SHARON'S SERVICE ***

Sharon sees much similarity between her ministry as a layperson and the ministry of the ordained – perhaps because of the types of responsibilities she carries. There are very few aspects of the running of the church that she does not participate in. The only exception is the celebration of the sacraments. The fact that she feels called to work in the service of God in the Church is, in her opinion, no different from the vocation that priests have to the priesthood. The calling, and the demand for integrity, are the same – and to Sharon the job and the ministry are the same.

She admits that her work would be much easier if she were able to administer the sacraments.

> The first example that comes to mind is being called to the hospital in the last minutes of someone's life. Many times the person wants to make a confession or have "the last rites" [sacrament of the sick]. I cannot always find a priest to administer these sacraments. How much easier and more meaningful it would be for everyone – patients and their families – if I were able to do this for them. In my opinion, it is a matter of acceptance.

Throughout the years, the people in her pastoral care have come to accept the larger role of women in their parish and in ministry in general. According to Sharon, it works well, even extremely well. "Perhaps if more people could come to this realization, how many more women would truly be able and allowed to live out their true calling."

*** MARLENE'S PERSPECTIVE ***

Marlene chooses her words carefully. She has given much thought to the factors that affect the comfort level priests have with her. In her experience, if a priest's main priority is the well-being of the people he serves, then he will welcome all the help he can get from lay ministers without feeling threatened by the pastoral minister's gifts and competence. Marlene works with ordained colleagues who affirm her ministry, and together they enjoy mutually supportive relationships, helping each other to grow in their ministries and learning from each other. Some of her closest friends are priests she has met over the years. In her words, "We are spiritual companions on the journey of ministry, and we provide one another with encouragement and personal support through the challenges and joys of our vocations."

At other times and with other priests, she has not been this fortunate. Sometimes a priest will passively or actively seek to undermine her efforts, her credibility, her integrity. She has experienced this several times. In one instance, a priest with whom she had the briefest acquaintance attempted to obstruct her ministry by questioning her sincerity and competence. Marlene was a threat simply because of the theology and ecclesiology she represented as a lay woman in ministry. She has had to conclude from such experiences that a priest seems most likely to feel threatened by a competent lay minister if he has unresolved personal issues with power and control, fear or insecurity, intimacy and sexuality.

Marlene has learned that even initial impressions can be deceiving. "Sometimes, even a priest who thinks of himself as very supportive of Vatican II will become oppressive and unjust in dealing with lay ministers if his own control issues come into play," she says.

Collaborative ministry works best if the priest and lay minister have at least some personal affinity for one another. It is very difficult to work with someone you don't care for. Marlene's best work is done with priests with whom she shares more than the task at hand. But even in the friendship sphere, the need for healthy boundaries and some level of emotional maturity is essential.

*** CARLA'S CONCERN ***

Carla raises a very different, but equally important, issue that distinguishes her ministry from that of the ordained. The demands of family life encroach on ministry. In her experience, children and the spouse of the pastoral minister are very exposed to the public eye. They feel pressured at times to be perfect because their wife or mom is in ministry. Carla is aware, from taking courses in non-Catholic theological colleges, how many ministers in other denominations have already struggled with this pressure. She herself wrestles with this as much as her family does.

"There is a fine line between how much one can be close friends with other families in the parish community and at the same time maintain a certain professional distance," she admits. This is especially difficult when you have lived in the community prior to the ministerial appointment.

On the other hand, she also sees a definite advantage in knowing something of the community and its dynamics before serving in a professional capacity. One must continually be on guard to maintain professionalism with families in the parish. "Just because my child associates with their child does not mean that I cannot minister to the family and maintain confidentiality," she says. "However, others don't mind dealing with me on both levels."

Carla adds that often the impact on family life of our work in ministry may not show up until months or years later. This is also the case for any job in the secular world that makes great demands of time and energy on the individual.

*

I have heard Carla's concerns voiced by clergy friends in other traditions. These concerns indeed build a strong argument in favour of celibate clergy, who do not have to deal with them. But when I consider my own experience of relationships with celibate Catholic priests and male ordained clergy from other traditions, I tend to think that the benefits are worth the added stresses on family life. Take for example my friend Rev'd Tim, an Anglican parish priest. Tim, who is married and the father of one child, is a great teacher and preacher, an organizer and a born leader. Over the years, we have collaborated in many ministries: ecumenical prayer events, my regular guest preaching in Sunday worship at his parish, workshops and retreats we facilitate together, pastoral care ventures and joint involvement in funerals. Our differences in personality, however, do not make for an easy relationship. Tim is thoughtful, with little spontaneous warmth; I am spontaneously warm, with thoughtfulness following much later. Tim is a meticulous thinker and scholar, and expresses compassion as a deliberate choice; I am naturally compassionate, think with my heart and feel with my head. On the surface, we look as incompatible as apples and oranges.

Tim and I have known times of great frustration as well as times of great collaboration. We have known times of anger and distance as well as times of genuine peer support, intimacy and respect. Nevertheless, our friendship is unlike any relationship I have with a

Catholic priest. Although it is impossible to establish cause and effect, I cannot help but wonder whether the durability of this friendship is a fruit of our married states. Does marriage, with both its good and its bad times, equip us for fruitful collaborative ministry despite our differences?

*** MILLIE'S CONTACTS ***

Millie studied theology for three years. During this time she formed many close friendships with seminarians with whom she maintains regular contact. At the same time she entered parish ministry for the first time, her seminarian friends were being ordained to the priesthood and starting out in their ministry as well.

Over and over, in their many discussions, Millie and her priest friends conclude that there are more similarities than differences in what they have chosen to do. Millie has found this to be true in what motivates and animates their ministry as well as in their theological base. They share the same frustrations, joys, doubts and loneliness. "Mind you, this should not be surprising," Millie reports, "given that we all took the same classes taught by the same professors. I do believe that this little subtlety gets forgotten – educationally we are all, seminarians and lay women, prepared for ministry by taking the same classes."

*** SHARON'S COLLABORATIONS ***

Sharon's best experiences of collaborative ministry have happened with priests who allowed her the freedom to do what was necessary wherever she ministered, and who could respect her for how she responds to people's needs. The most painful part is that some of the men she has worked with are what she calls "lone rangers." When I ask her what she means by that, she explains that such priests feel accountable to no one, and so they have very little need or willingness to consult with others. Sharon elaborates:

> This morning I had exactly the experience I have had many times over. I had just made an appointment to bring one of our sick parishioners communion. After Mass, the priest requested that a couple show him where this person lived. I told Father that I was on my way there, and was expected later on.

However, he insisted that he would bring her communion now, and that he would go unannounced.

In this case Sharon declined to go. She has to choose her battles, and did not want to fight this one. Sadly, incidents like this one occur too frequently for her. "Our men seem to feel they have every right to usurp another's plans without consideration," she says.

*

Rev. Donald Cozzens has written amply in several books about what Sharon is describing here.[17] Cozzens begins Chapter 7 of *Sacred Silence* with a quote from Alexander Schmemann, a renowned Orthodox theologian and seminary dean:

> Clericalism suffocates; it makes part of itself into the whole sacred character of the Church; it makes its power a sacred power to control, to lead, to administer; a power to perform sacraments, and, in general it makes any power a 'power given to me.'[18]

*** LENORA'S INSIGHTS ***

Once again, Lenora offers some thoughtful, yet troubling, insights.

> My time of studying alongside seminarians was both affirming and challenging. Academically I proved my competency, and I was recognized as their equal. But I experienced, in my friendships with some young men, that they learned early in their formation to split off the sexual part of their personhood in order to accommodate the celibate requirement of their priestly calling.

I look concerned, and ask her to be specific.

> Some of them clearly displayed "courting" behaviour toward me, and I'm not referring to my now husband. When I confronted a seminarian about his courting behaviour out loud, he vehemently denied having any feelings for me and said it was all in my head.

Playing devil's advocate, I ask Lenora whether he might have been right and she had misinterpreted the signs. She becomes defensive, and her dark eyes glow.

I'm a grown woman. I can tell when a man makes advances. I'm not sure who he was kidding, me or himself. It seems that splitting off a part of his being and projecting it onto others, onto women in particular, was easier than facing the pain of giving up the notion of ever sharing his sexuality with a woman in the intimate expression of human love and physical union.

I agree with Lenora that our human sexuality is very powerful. Whether we are celibate or married, heterosexual or homosexual, we have a responsibility to integrate and live in harmony with this wild fire inside of us, a fire that "comes from the gods," as Fr. Ron Rolheiser has described it.[19] Just as some married men have difficulty remaining faithful, obligatory celibacy seems to make some men (not all) choose not to own their sexuality at all instead of integrating it in healthy ways. As Cozzens' recent writings have illustrated, failure to integrate one's sexuality can diminish celibacy as a charism. Lenora's experience does not seem to be an isolated one. In any case, it has made her very concerned about how celibate priests will relate to women in their parish ministries, and especially to women collaborators in ministry.

*** GLADYS'S ISSUE ***

For the most part, collaborative ministry has been favourable for Gladys. This is the only way in which the parishes could possibly function up north, however.

One source of pain or struggle for Gladys centres on how a certain problem can surface within the parish.

Several priests who were here for week-long stints were consulted on what should be done to resolve a certain issue. I was not consulted, even though I had brought the problem to the powers that be and I am the one who is, here on a daily basis. It was one of the few times that I felt that the old boys' club had closed ranks against me.

This type of incident made Gladys feel that for the daily running of the parish she was fine, but when there was something substantial to be decided, as a woman she had nothing to offer to the discussion. This was extremely hurtful to her.

Despite the fact that she feels invisible within the larger church organization, Gladys thinks that being able to administer the sacraments would greatly benefit her ministry. While she is able to do funerals, she finds that she could do far more for those who are dying if she could administer the sacrament of the sick or hear confessions. Although most people prefer to wait for a priest to have their children baptized or to get married. several have asked her to give their children their First Communion.

> While I teach them the classes for this sacrament and do the whole sacramental preparation, the administration of the actual sacrament has to be done by a priest. It seems a little silly to me that although I distribute communion at Mass and am the sole distributor at communion services, I am unable to give them the Eucharist for the first time.

*** DEANNA'S STYLE ***

Deanna, in her usual blunt style, which endears her to the inmates to whom she ministers, thinks that the Church may have a shortage of male priests, but that there is no shortage of vocations or pastors. She believes that it's time for the Church to reflect both the feminine and masculine face of God in its pastoral leaders, much in the same way as the Holy Father speaks about the need for the Church to "breathe with two lungs" when he refers to the Eastern and the Western traditions of Christianity. As Deanna says,

> The world is starving for authentic witness. It seems that in the western hemisphere, God has raised up an army of middle-aged women to show the way to the two faces of pastoral leadership needed in our day — male and female.

*** MILLIE'S CALLING ***

While most of us in pastoral ministry tend not to place ourselves in any political or feminist camps on the question of women's ordination, dealing with pastoral needs and the reality of the shortage of priests on a daily basis forces us to face the supposedly "forbidden" questions. Millie, gentle and middle-aged, has no doubt about her calling.

We are all God's people, male and female, capable of doing whatever God asks of us with his help and guidance. How can the Church restrict whom God chooses to call? I become very annoyed when gender becomes a negative factor in how my ministry is evaluated. This attitude shows up most strongly when I attend gatherings for pastoral ministers and I am the subject of suspicious looks from ordained presbyters.

She considers her calling or vocation to be the same as that of a priest, although she lives this vocation as a lay minister. Whereas the education of a priest is most instrumental in forming and informing him, Millie's life experiences as a woman, a spouse, a mother and a professional in the workplace form and inform her ministry. She is aware that her calling is also more complex and multi-faceted than that of a priest, but not necessarily less important or inferior.

*

I am relieved. By and large, many of us report good relationships with priests. But as can happen in any hierarchical setting, some priests seem to consider themselves superior to lay people by virtue of their ordination. The clericalism and hierarchical ordering of church leadership fosters an unhealthy distance between the ordained and non-ordained. According to Donald Cozzens, this fosters an inordinate sense of entitlement in the ordained.[20] The respect lay people have for the priest then becomes more based on the hierarchical understanding of the priesthood than upon respect earned by the personal integrity and care by the priest in his ministry.

Several women observe that clericalism is often communicated through the priest's body language and manner of speaking. For some men, authority seems derived primarily from their institutional status as ordained ministers. Less care and attention are given to establishing their authority in the hearts of the people they serve.

A lot of damage can occur as a result of an attitude of entitlement. Parishioners can get hurt or turned off. When people do not receive respect, or when their ideas and contributions are not truly listened to, they may simply quit coming. In most of these cases, they may not have abandoned the Catholic faith, but rather their sense of community and belonging has failed to be sustained.

*** A GAMUT OF EXPERIENCES ***

Francine has experienced the whole gamut of possible relationships with ordained ministers – from falling deeply in love with individual priests to being verbally and sexually abused by others. In her experience, relationships between male ordained ministers and female, especially single, lay ministers, rarely remain neutral. For Francine, any discussion of male–female dynamics cannot be separated from the patriarchal power dynamic within the institutional Church, a dynamic that renders the female presence in general, and in a ministerial role in particular, invisible and her voice mute.

> Whether the relationship between male ordained minister and female lay minister is positive or negative, the fact remains that there is an imbalance of power inherent within the very structures of the Church. As such, true collaborative ministry becomes almost impossible to achieve.

There is another obstacle that Francine experiences in her attempts to work collaboratively with celibate clergy and to develop healthy male–female dynamics in ministry. She senses a strong overall reticence within Catholic culture itself when it comes to articulating our sexuality. This is true for Catholic couples, and it is true for celibate priests. The few priests Francine has grown close to have shared with her on occasion about the challenges of living a celibate lifestyle.

> From talking to priests, I know that many struggle with celibacy, yet it remains taboo to bring this struggle to the fore. Because the struggle is forced to the unconscious, a priest may express it in negative ways within the male–female dynamics when he attempts to work in a pastoral team.

Even in the rare case when the male experience is articulated, the female experience (the injustice faced by women within these relationships) still remains largely ignored, Francine believes. When a female pastoral minister has a good collaborative relationship with a priest, it should come as no surprise that sexual feelings and attractions may emerge in each one periodically. If such attractions fail to be openly acknowledged, named and contained (with or without both parties), they may be suppressed, denied or grow out of proportion, thus playing havoc with the ministry relationship. Francine knows from personal experience how explosive such situations can become. She has often wondered where and how women can find a voice to articulate the complexity of experience when it comes to relating to the celibate male ordained minister. What's more, there are non-ordained men, married and single, working in pastoral ministry who report similar problems and tensions in their relationships to the ordained. We women are not the only ones.

When my daughter was a teenager and learned all about boys, I asked her once how she "knows" which boys are worthy of her time and attention and which ones are not. She was surprised by my question, and thought that I had asked because I could not tell the difference. "Mom, don't you know that yet?! I just, you know, 'know.' Something inside tells me. If they treat me with respect and can take no for an answer without getting all bent out of shape, then I have a pretty good idea of how mature they are." I laughed, and was reassured. And I recognized her reliance on intuition, even though she did not use that word.

I, too, rely on intuition when it comes to relating to men, and to celibate ordained presbyters in particular. I have called it the need to exercise a kind of "sixth sense." I have worked with priests who are secure within themselves and have a healthy self-esteem. Such men are emotionally and mentally free to relate as equals in ministry. With them, true collaboration is possible; the experience of ministry is effective and becomes a source of great joy.

It is no longer a secret, however, that some priests struggle with celibacy and fail to achieve a healthy integration of their sexuality. Authors such as Donald Cozzens, Eugene Kennedy, Richard Sipe and Andrew Greeley have written amply about factors in the priest's psychosexual makeup that can make the vow of celibacy a complicated burden, even to the point of inappropriate sexual behaviour, regardless of whether the priest is heterosexual or homosexual. In Kennedy's words,

One of the problems of dwelling in a less than healthy clerical world is the denial implicit in that world. It is often unspoken but nonetheless present and creates an unnecessary gulf of social connecting necessary for effective pastoral care and preaching. [Assumptions] which easily lead to an attitude of entitlement and an exaggerated sense of being special set the priest up for all manner of falls.[21]

If such internal conflict and ambivalence are not acknowledged on a conscious level, they find expression in projection onto the very people who trigger the priest's ambivalence: women. Sometimes this projection is blatant, but most often it is subtle, indirect and non-verbal. Unacknowledged issues with one's sexuality often result in missed opportunities for effective collaborative ministry.

I have had meetings with clergy in which my contributions were subtly, or not so subtly, ignored for no apparent reason. I have heard that priests have spoken behind my back using pejorative terms about women in ministry – and somehow this always gets back to the person in question in a roundabout way. Sometimes a priest has adopted a patronizing tone of voice when speaking to me. I have often wondered what goes on inside a priest who behaves as if I were not there or who prefers to give me orders rather than consult. I have tried to understand such behaviour with good will and concern. Why do some men seem threatened by women like me in a ministerial role? These experiences fill me with more sadness than anger.

*** LENORA'S COURAGE ***

Lenora has attended several of her classmates' ordinations to the priesthood. These are always occasions of great happiness as well as sadness for her. She is happy for her friend being ordained, and rejoices that he receives the Church's affirmation of who God has called him to become. At the same time, she feels the injustice at being barred from the same recognition. She explains how her seminarian friends have access to the Church's support and guidance to discern and test their calling. Her need for a similar discernment, however, is recognized only if her calling is to religious life. Lenora tells me, "Helping a woman to discern a call to ministry is not a service the

Catholic Church provides." Women like Lenora are left to their own devices to figure it out. She admits that this is painful, and that she suffers from this lack of support and guidance. "Who will help me discern my calling?" she wonders.

But even though the Church does not know how to accommodate the need women have to discern their calling into ministry, God's Spirit calls women in unexpected, creative and persistent ways. And the Spirit of Jesus has always initiated new things that the Church has often accepted only reluctantly and long after the fact. This is most aptly illustrated by the stormy beginnings of several religious orders. Lenora draws courage from the foundresses of certain religious orders for women, such as Clare of Assisi, Teresa of Avila and Mary Ward, "and the difficulties they experienced in obtaining recognition for their innovative approaches."

I ask Lenora whether she considers her calling as being similar to that of a priest. She replies,

> My calling is both the same as and different from that of an ordained priest. I live out my calling as a lay person, which is the only expression open to me. I do not vow obedience to my local bishop in the same way as ordained presbyters do. My relationship to the bishop is not as clearly defined, but also does not bind me in the same way. Also, my ecclesial mandate is not permanent nor attached to me as a person, but is primarily tied to the function I fulfill.

She rightly adds that these differences are liberating as well as stifling, a source of both joy and deep sorrow. They are liberating and joyful since they give her freedom to move and to be creative in her ministry. They are stifling and sorrowful since she sorely misses the Church's formal blessing, protection and support, which ordination provides.

*

I wonder about Lenora's sense of call. Does she want to be ordained? Why? Is ordination about some external validation or about feeling good? In our culture of self-help and feel-good psychology, it is important to distinguish psychological from vocational reasons for ordination. Our vocation refers to that way of being in the world (and in the Church) that taps our deepest and fullest human potential. Once we discover and embrace our vocation, whatever that is, we know that fullness of life lies in the recognition of that vocation. To fulfill life's potential, we cannot do anything else but embrace God's call. Is it possible for a woman to feel called to ordained ministry?

I keep dreaming of the possibility of collaborative ministry between ordained and lay ministers, between male and female leadership in the Church. I work in a diocese and with a bishop who encourages such an inclusive vision in creative yet faithful ways. I am amazed at the power that even the vision of inclusiveness and collaboration itself can exercise on those in ministry. "Without a vision, the people perish," says the author of Proverbs (29:18, King James Version). A vision dictates what we are blind to and what we see as possibilities. A vision fuels motivation and taps energy, concentrating it in those places we consider important.

Even though the vision drives our actions, more often than not we run into the human condition of sinfulness and shortcomings. In our dealings with one another, we bump into the unhealed lives of both priests and lay people. Our inadequate relating is often the cause of strife, anger, alienation and deep pain. Collaboration in ministry is hard work.

Sometimes, I catch life-giving glimpses of the vision. Concluding a joint workshop one day, Fr. Daniel and I looked at one another with gratitude and satisfaction. "We did it!" We laughed and gave one another a thumbs-up. When collaborative ministry is allowed to be a forceful witness, it reveals more fully the radical equality of the Gospel of Jesus Christ to the people of God.

> There is no longer Jew or Greek, there is no longer slave or free, there is no longer male and female; for all of you are one in Christ Jesus. (Galatians 3:28)

7

Woman, Why Are You Weeping?

Daughters of Jerusalem,
do not weep for me,
but weep for yourselves and for your children.

(Luke 23:28)

Pastoral ministry can be extremely wearying. Most parishioners have no idea how lonely the position can be. Even though meeting the pastoral needs of the church family brings me into contact with many people, the nature and quality of those contacts demand much discretion, energy and concentration. It is the kind of focused attention to the human encounter that can leave me depleted afterwards. Much of the work is of a confidential nature – I have nowhere to go to unburden myself other than to Jesus in prayer.

As a lay ecclesial minister, I come from among the people. Yet I am also set apart to provide pastoral leadership. To be both of the people and separate from them can create frustration and misunderstandings on both sides. Parishioners are unsure about how to relate to me; for me, exercising leadership and at the same time being one of the community is a fine balance. Pastoral responsibilities and having to be available all the time can be overwhelming. I have gained a greater appreciation of the burden of parish leadership carried by our priests. While people look up to priests and admire them for what they do, most people have no idea how to situate and support me. It's hard for parishioners to show empathy or understanding; the stakes are high.

*** SHARON'S EYE-OPENER ***

Being a parish administrator has been an eye-opener for Sharon. She sees self-care as the biggest issue lurking in the background. "I don't really know how our priests survive year after year doing this job, with very little support and very little nurturing of their spirits," she says. "This is the ideal place for burnout and I am always conscious of that!"

*** AUDREY'S PAIN ***

Audrey has cried herself to sleep more than once because of the lonely nature of her own vocational discernment. She has now found a creative expression of her vocation in hospital chaplaincy. Nevertheless, she keeps wondering, and has asked God, why God calls while the Church refuses to mandate her calling in any formal way. It is her very study of Catholic theology and social teaching, of Catholic anthropology and sacramental understanding, that has awakened her call to ministry. She knows from personal experience that women are not a stop-gap measure to deal with the priest shortage; God is bestowing a call of our own on us all – women and men.

*

There is so much wisdom in gifted women that is being ignored, wasted and undervalued in the face of the Church's own best insights. The Church's limited vision has not stopped God from calling women and helping them to find fruitful expressions of their vocation, however. In the face of this reality, the institutional invisibility of women in pastoral ministry (there is no formal mandate, no job security, no formal protection, and no formal blessing) creates a painful crucible of suffering. As one woman said, it's like Jesus being rejected in his own hometown. "The only place I can take this pain is to Jesus on the cross – there I find understanding, support and consolation."

*** LENORA'S SHADOW ***

As mentioned earlier, Lenora's previous bishop gave her a mandate to celebrate baptisms, weddings and funerals. However life-giving it was to Lenora to facilitate the human–divine sacramental encounter, the people's and the Church's preoccupations with external issues cast a shadow over her ministry.

> Given that my empowerment to serve in some kind of sacramental way was not considered at all normal, I constantly had to explain why I was serving this way, and found that nearly everyone had a very strong opinion about it, either supportive or disapproving. The stress that accompanied the mandate was considerable, as I felt it made me a lightning rod for the larger questions facing our Church.

Even though Lenora herself did not directly engage in discussions on the thorny issues of women in pastoral leadership, her very witness in pastoral ministry was enough to provoke the "forbidden" questions. She adds,

> I also was aware of being branded as a radical simply for serving as the bishop had asked me to. I was aware that I was serving in a symbolic way and was receiving a lot of projections from people, both positive and negative. Prayer was a key to helping me hold on to my own sense of self in the midst of these projections.

With a change in bishops, however, Lenora's mandate for baptisms and weddings has effectively been suspended. This has been a relief of sorts. It freed her from being the centre of controversy, even though she finds it disappointing to have to explain to Catholics in the university community that she can no longer witness weddings.

> It is even more frustrating when the couple cannot find a priest who is available and willing to witness their wedding. Their experience of Church becomes negative when priests treat them with impatience or disrespect. In this case, my ministry is hampered and many people end up not receiving the ministry they need.

Several months after our initial conversations, Lenora contacted me again. The bishop in her diocese now showed himself to be far from supportive of lay ecclesial ministers in pastoral and parish appointments. Lenora had lost her job. I asked her what this meant for her and her love for ministry. "I guess I'll have to find work elsewhere.

What this means for my call to ministry, I don't even want to think about right now." I heard the pain in her voice.

*

It is not hard to identify with the kind of pain Sharon, Audrey and Lenora express. Even though recent studies show that the number of lay ecclesial ministers continues to increase,[22] women as paid professionals in ministry are still an anomaly in the Catholic community of faith. Often, emotions and reactions, both positive and negative, run high.

I worked in a parish once as a pastoral associate. My responsibilities included facilitating all aspects of adult faith formation, RCIA and outreach to young families, as well as initiating a process of evaluation for liturgical ministries. The parish had had numerous volunteers serving in a variety of ministries. Even though the need for overall coordination and guidance was evident, employing a lay person in a ministerial role evoked mixed feelings. A delicate balancing act was required between my professional responsibilities and the volunteers' areas of ministry. My position was not created to take away what parishioners were doing on a voluntary basis, but to strengthen, guide and feed their energy and creativity. However, parish volunteers had difficulty grasping this, and some saw their territory invaded by professionalism.

During my short stay in this parish, many new people came forward willing to get involved. At the same time, there was much resistance from those who were long-standing and faithful "pillars" of the parish. They preferred the status quo over making changes for new parishioners to feel welcome. The priest was new to our country and needed all his energy just to adapt to the culture. Moreover, he didn't relate well to women in leadership, which seriously complicated the situation.

Despite the fact that the parish council hired me, neither the parish at large nor the pastor was able or willing to take ownership of my ministerial presence. This seriously jeopardized two of the three sources of authority necessary when exercising ministry (see

Chapter 4): the institutional mandate and the endorsement from the people. Once enough new members had joined the parish council, my one-year contract was broken after six months, with only three days' notice. I asked the chair of the parish council if my professional conduct had been questionable. "No, on the contrary," he said, "you worked within the mandate you were given. Possibly you were too good at the job and some parishioners couldn't handle that." As he looked away from me, his voice trailed off as if losing confidence. He continued, "Maybe the parish wasn't ready for someone like you. I'm sorry." I got the distinct impression that he felt caught in the middle of an odd and dysfunctional crossfire.

I felt profoundly betrayed and rejected. Given my understanding of ministry, I had entered a covenant with the parish that extended far beyond just doing a job. I had trusted that the parish at large would take ownership of my role in pastoral ministry – and it did not. The priest could not look me in the eye when I left. I admit that healing is ongoing.

The meeting with my spiritual director that followed this event was filled with painful tears. Honouring the pain, he nevertheless said gently, "God is waiting eagerly to teach you many things through this experience – when you are ready." It was all I could do to stay soft and pliable in God's arms, and not to bury myself in bitterness, anger and utter despair.

*** FRANCINE'S PAIN ***

Francine's source of pain also lies with the faith community itself, but she articulates it in a different way. She senses that her desire for the people to grow in faith is far greater than their own desire.

> If only they could taste the sweetness of a faith rich with God's presence in Jesus! Yet most seem to settle for mediocrity, with a minimal connection to the Church. Then, when a crisis hits, they come knocking on the door in despair, but with few inner resources of faith. It's a bit like trying to serve people steak and lobster when all they want is hot dogs. I used to cry a lot for myself; now I cry for others and their refusal of Christ's invitation to the fullness of life. Too many people in the pews are satisfied with mediocrity, which in turn can

kill passion and enthusiasm in others. Too many times I've been on fire about Scripture, about learning theology, about inviting others to share and learn along with me, only to be met with polite indifference.

Sometimes when parishioners do try to gather to pray and learn together, Francine reports, their actions are viewed with suspicion and the initiative does not last long. "It does not help that the demands of family life and children's commitments (sports, lessons, etc.) seem to take priority in most families' timetables," she adds.

*** SHARON'S SHADOW ***

For Sharon, parish ministry is exciting, fulfilling and a great avenue to use her gifts. At the same time, it is lonely, isolating and frustrating. There are so many parts of her job as administrator that have nothing to do with God's reign. There are so many demands that take no account of who or how she is as a person.

> Days off can be interrupted by calls to the hospital, death of a parishioner, crisis in a household, and the expectation is that you be there. As administrator, I find that many people do not respect boundaries. Many holidays are work days and often it is hard to recoup them, as the work of the parish continues.

Celebration of the sacraments and of the Eucharist can be difficult at times. Sharon is the one who prepares the people and the celebration, and she takes great care to do a good job. But sometimes the ordained presider comes in and makes changes without consulting or informing her. She finds this very painful. In particular, she has a hard time with the way the Eucharist is celebrated. "I feel that if women were to be presiders, some of the ritual parts would need to change, as women celebrate differently from men," she tells me. "Fewer words, perhaps, and more emphasis on symbol."

*** GLADYS'S SORROW ***

Not all women in ministry note the same sources of pain. Women in the north, particularly, have greater freedom in how they exercise their ministry. They also enjoy greater respect from, and better collaboration with, their bishop, who is acutely aware of his need for such dedicated lay ministers. The visiting priests who provide sacramental ministry do not try to be absentee pastors, and the parishioners, the vast majority being First Nations people, regard the women as competent and trustworthy pastors.

For this reason, Gladys reports a sorrow of an entirely different sort. I have included her experience as a reminder that our sources of pain are not all the same, but indeed can be many.

In the northern village where Gladys runs the parish, there are two other churches: Full Gospel and Bible Fellowship. The former was started about 20 years ago by a couple of families from the community. They bring in evangelical preachers from time to time, and Gladys has been told that there has been open talk against the Catholic Church. The couple in charge is friendly towards Gladys, but she has heard testimonies beginning, "I am Christian. I used to be Catholic." While the memorials or vigils are in the Full Gospel Church, nearly all the funerals are in the context of the Mass in the Catholic Church. This creates serious tensions. Gladys is filled with sadness that so many people do not know the faith in which they were raised. "Even those who attend our church are very weak in understanding matters of faith," she says.

The Bible Fellowship in Gladys's community is led by a very devoted American couple who have lived there for over 20 years. They are friendly to Gladys and the three of them have been involved in various community events together. When Gladys once asked for a meeting of the church leaders to see what they could do together for the community, the meeting was pleasant. They decided to meet once each week for united prayer for the village. A few people from the Full Gospel joined those at the Catholic Church at the beginning, but the Bible Fellowship leader did not attend. "Vast theological differences make it impossible to pray together," he explained.

Gladys continues,

> Two years ago, I invited the leaders of each of these churches to consider participating in training for the Alpha Course. The training weekend had to be cancelled, as not enough participants could be available on the given date.

> Last December, the Bible Fellowship began Alpha in our town. I saw posters inviting the community at large, but there had been no communication with our parish regarding the planning. Hence, I feel that there is a distrust of the Catholic Church and that some of the local people have bought into that.

Gladys struggles with the so-called fundamentalist Christian churches and fellowships vying for the minds and hearts of First Nations people, even though such churches sometimes condemn First Nations' cultural and spiritual practices. By doing so they end up repeating errors made earlier by colonizing churches. Meanwhile, "our Catholic church looks on, unaware of its loss of large numbers of people," Gladys comments with regret in her voice.

Gladys claims that fundamentalist interpretation of Christian faith, and the subsequent pressure to abandon Native spirituality, has resulted in suicides. As well as condemning Native cultures, some fundamentalist groups condemn the Catholic Church, Gladys explains. According to her, some of these groups have a very active mission to "convert" Catholics away from their church. Meanwhile, Gladys asks: "And what are we, the Catholic Church, doing by way of evangelizing our own people?"

*** AT ODDS ***

Carla feels strangely at odds with the institutional Church. The Church that causes the most pain is the same Church that gives her the authority to minister. Her official professional ministry is tied wholly to that same Church. Even while her ministry has been within the Roman Catholic Church, her self-identity is not. She struggles with the Church's teachings and its example, and often wonders why she remains a part of this institution.

"When I think of abandoning it, my heart is torn, though," she says, "and I am still in the process of figuring out why, and what I'll ultimately do about it." She feels that her ministry has been one big apology. She claims that she constantly feels forced to defend her calling and her right to serve in ministry to most of the clergy who come to celebrate Mass and other sacraments, as well as to those people who do not accept her ministry as valid.

Carla detests making this a male–female issue, but others force her to do so almost all the time. "I believe that harmony and collaboration are not only possible, but absolutely necessary if we are to live as Jesus taught us," she tells me. "Meanwhile, I live with the pain."

*

Carla's words echo in my own heart and mind. Being a part of the institutional Church is a strange phenomenon. Sometimes it feels like a mother–child relationship that refuses to move to an adult–adult rapport. Like a good parent and mother, the Church desires and urges her children to grow and mature in their faith. In the case of my own parents, they insisted on us all attending Sunday Mass every week when we were growing up. Once I discovered on my own, when I was in my teens, that following Jesus was about much more than simply showing up at Mass on Sunday, they were convinced I had "overdosed" on religion. Like my parents, the Church is often ambivalent when we grow and mature in faith.

A significant portion of church members seem to remain "adult children," passive consumers of sacraments with little need to grow a deeper understanding of their faith. Then there are those who stop participating but nevertheless classify themselves as Catholic (sociologist Reginald Bibby calls such people "affiliates"[23]) and will turn to the Church for baptisms, marriages and funerals. My own parents now fall into this category. When they celebrated their 50th wedding anniversary, their latent Catholic connection led them to celebrate this with a Mass, even though the parish priest didn't even know them because they never attend on Sundays. In a recent conversation, my mother admitted that she had never learned about a personal relationship to God, and that "church" for her remained confined to rules and observances with little substance.

Finally, there are those who develop their Christian discipleship as the centre of their lives (the ones that "overdose," according to my mother). They grow a deep faith and cherish strong participation in the life of the parish. Some of these women and men eventually claim desires and callings indicating that ministry is meant to become their primary expression of who they are. However, that same "Mother

Church" seems reluctant to affirm and bless the very outcomes of the maturing process it has so encouraged, unless the call is awakened in a celibate man. Women who claim such callings have simply taken seriously, and obediently followed, the Church's command to deepen our relationship to God through Jesus in prayer, study and the celebration of the sacraments. It is our very obedience and commitment that lead to the discovery that God calls.

It is one thing to awaken to our most passionate desire to serve the people of God in ecclesial ministry; it is another to minister out of those passions and desires, and then to be treated with suspicion and distrust for doing so. The resistance and invisibility within the institution that so many women in ministry face create a unique, deep pain that, if not surrendered in prayer and joined to Jesus, can eat away at self-esteem and self-confidence, energy for ministry, and even trust in God's guidance. Sometimes the pain is so deep that anger and bitterness take root in our hearts, forcing us to consider a career outside the Church. Paradoxically, the pain we suffer in ministry, if carried honestly, gently and surrendered to Jesus in prayer, also has the power to authenticate our calling.

*** MILLIE'S REJECTIONS ***

Take Millie's experience.

> I have experienced rejection. I can remember participating in a lay-presided liturgy where I preached for the first time. I was complimented by a deacon on my reflection. A priest whom I really respect was somewhat put off by this and said, "Well, you'll never be ordained, honey!" Coming from him, it hurt, but I got over it.

> Another time, when I was a lay presider, two people walked out of the church when they realized I was not a priest.

Instead of discouraging her, these types of reactions make Millie more determined to remain part of the new face of ministry for the sake of the Church's own well-being and future.

*** FRANCINE'S MEMORIES ***

In her diocesan work, Francine has painful memories of a similar nature. She has experienced pain and frustration over incompetent leadership – both male priests and female traditional leaders – that gets in the way of good adult faith formation.

> I remember the last Chrism Mass I attended – I had been invited to read the first reading and I had memorized it, wanting to proclaim it from my heart. And I did. But my heart was soon deflated when the bishop gave his homily. He stated the parameters – male and celibate – on who could be called by God. I knew as I walked away that night that I would probably never attend another Chrism Mass again. I know in my heart of hearts that God does not have such parameters. It frustrates me when a person's sex dictates their role and not their gifts.

Again, rather than walking away from the challenges, Francine is even more motivated to be part of the solution in ministry. The ways we respond and appropriate the painful experiences in ministry – an unavoidable testing ground, it seems! – can become authenticating markers of the divine nature of our calling. This is not easy, and the temptation to become bitter and disillusioned is very big. Good mentorship with a spiritual director or peer support group with other women in ministry (or both) can provide essential ways for ongoing reflection, guidance and encouragement.

*** MARLENE'S LOVE ***

Marlene used to say that she loves the Church – but she doesn't like that expression anymore because it sounds too uncritical. Marlene compares her love for the Church with the love she has for her spouse.

> When I said to Bill that I would choose to love him forever, I meant it. I knew that this included loving his warts and shortcomings. I knew that the challenges we would have would be part of that choice to love him. I think I love the Church kind of like that – I know it is not perfect, that there are things about it that cause me great pain. The Church has a lot of maturing to do, but I love it just the same.

Marlene wishes the Church would do a better job at walking the Gospel talk of inclusiveness. She wishes that criteria for leadership in the Church would include passion, competence and giftedness, not gender. Nevertheless, Marlene would rather live with the kinks and imperfections of the current faith tradition than deal with the surprises of a different Christian tradition. She would rather stay and transform the Church from within than watch it from a distance.

"I believe that as long as I keep Jesus central, anything is possible," she says, "including working in a Church that often chooses to be blind to the pain it causes."

*** ANNETTE'S PAIN ***

Annette now works as a pastoral associate in a western Canadian city. Despite the difficult relationship she has with the parish priest, she derives satisfaction and joy from her ministry. She recalls her most painful experience, when she still lived in the United States. After sixteen years, Annette chose to leave religious life while remaining part of the same parish where she taught in the parochial school and was heavily involved in various aspects of parish life. The majority of the people accepted her decision, respected her, and continued to see her as a friend and active member of the parish. Some, however, suddenly rejected her as a person and as a parishioner the moment she was no longer "Sister." She recalls what happened.

> I chaired the liturgy committee at the time and, while most supported me in this position, some now took the opportunity to question my background in liturgy, my decision-making authority and even my opinion.

One of the most hurtful situations involved a choir that Annette had directed for a few years as a sister and now continued directing as a layperson. After the choir's usual summer break, she overheard that a new director had been hired – a non-Catholic professional musician whom she knew was excellent but who had no background in liturgical music and would now get a salary for something Annette had done as a volunteer.

When she inquired why her assistance was no longer wanted, most responded that someone had told them that she didn't have time to direct anymore.

> Parishioners were angry when the truth of the situation was finally revealed, and promises were made at a reconciliation meeting. It took quite a while to heal and to feel reconciled so I could again attend Masses at which this choir sang, especially when some parishioners informed me that I was not allowed to sing along!

*** BEING FEMALE ***

Wylma does not have to think long to identify her source of pain in the Church: being a female in ministry.

> I have often found myself marginalized by the men of the Church, both lay and ordained. I have longed to be understood and to experience collaborative ministry. Understanding has not been forthcoming except for one or two notable exceptions. Only in one instance was it unequivocal.

For Wylma, collaborative ministry has not really happened, other than within her own missionary community. In their team of two, and now three, they have been forced to work on their own, without a clear connection of shared ministry with the Church at large. Collaborative ministry with priests has been minimal, and mostly non-existent. That in itself has been a source of pain and struggle.

Darlene adds that she has seen little understanding of pastoral ministry as a real team project. This has had an impact on their ministry to First Nations people in an urban setting. "When a parish priest believes he is collaborating," she says, "he really simply sends our way the situations he cannot deal with."

With regard to the lack of collaboration with the clergy, it is difficult to trace the origins of some attitudes or approaches. Wylma and Darlene venture some questions: "Do they stem from a sense that men are innately superior to women? Are they caused by unresolved sexuality and intimacy issues? Or do certain priests have a need to 'hide' behind their collar?" Regardless of what the answer is, to a laywoman the answer to each of these questions manifests itself in much the same way. This phenomenon can prevent much-needed teamwork and can seriously hinder the spread of God's reign.

By contrast, Wylma notes that the First Nations people truly honour and respect her. They see her and her ministry partners primarily as people of prayer, relating to them with remarkable trust and openness, and with the utmost respect. In contrast, the larger mainstream church community sees the women's Native ministry as marginal, with the exception of a handful of individuals who understand their ministry and even support it financially. "In general," she says, "there seems to be a distinct discomfort, not so much with us as persons, but with the ministry we represent, with our association with the 'poor' and 'Native.'"

Often, people admire Wylma and her ministry partners for their work, and will make remarks such as, "I could never …"; at the same time, they do not know what their ministry entails and have no sense of who the people they serve really are.

> Our real ministry is not seen or understood, let alone shared, because the church community in our area has not reached a comfort level with First Nations people. Ironically and curiously, for many in the Aboriginal community we are regarded as a link to the Church and represent the larger faith community.

*** WYLMA'S RESPONSE ***

It is very painful to accept how slowly the Church moves on the things that need changing. Maybe this perception flows only from looking at ministry and Church from too human a perspective. Wylma's response to her call has been lived out in the context of a religious order (seven years) and a diocesan church (21 years), and, in particular, in ministry to First Nations people for a total of 30 years now.

In those 30 years, however, Wylma believes that many opportunities for making ministry more effective and more extensive have simply been lost. To maintain freshness, enthusiasm and vision in this context is a major challenge, particularly as she has now served several generations of the same families in her own lifetime. "The people could be so much better served with a more imaginative and more collaborative approach," she says. In many ways, she sees the Aboriginal community and those doing ministry among First Nations people as the "orphans" of Mother Church. I comment that this is quite a strong statement. She means it, and does not retract it.

Wylma expected change to take time with Aboriginal people. In her experience, First Nations people's slowness is a reflection of their patience. At the same time, they eagerly welcome whatever authentic ministry is offered in their midst. What she finds more frustrating and less excusable are the Church's delays and neglect. The exception seems to be the Church in the far north, about which Wylma reads and hears, but has not visited. In her experience, Native ministry appears on the annual agenda of a parish, deanery or diocese from time to time, and is then shelved again until the next occasion.

The Church's ministry to First Nations people moves painfully and unnecessarily slowly, she tells me. "The people live and the people die, with a higher than average death rate from violence, suicide, despair and addiction. My only comfort is God's word: 'I myself will shepherd them' [Ezekiel 34:15]."

Wylma struggles with the hiddenness of her ministry. At one level, she now realizes that this is within God's design, for reasons she can fathom only dimly. She does not want recognition, but she often longs to be part of a much larger ministry team or community where many can consciously share gifts and talents for building the kingdom of God. At the same time, she understands herself to be part of a large network of such people, without the consolation of knowing who or where they are.

*

As the experiences shared in this book reveal, I have encountered uplifting, courageous and hopeful stories of Catholic women in ministry, but I have also heard particularly painful accounts. In one week I had extensive phone conversations with two women, each in a different province. Each had been a pastoral associate in her parish for a number of years. From their own accounts, I concluded that their ministries were fruitful and appreciated by parishioners and pastors alike. Both women reported good relations with their parish's ordained pastor and worked well with him.

In the past year, each parish had seen a change of pastors. In both cases, the new pastor intended to eliminate the women's positions as pastoral associate without due reason, other than his unwillingness to work with a pastoral associate. As I listened on the phone, I heard their pain and frustration. By the time I began writing this book, both women had been fired and were not replaced. For at least one of them, this was not the first time.

> A few years ago, I was in another ministry situation where prolonged conflict in a parish zapped morale and energy. There was so much turmoil and internal fighting that I wanted to leave after six months. Many times I cried myself to sleep. I was underpaid, taxed emotionally and spiritually, and had no other job prospects.

The other woman was so discouraged that she wondered about looking for work in a non-church environment. When I asked her, "What does this mean for your own calling to ministry?" she replied, "Don't ask right now. It hurts too much."

It is our love for God in the person of Jesus Christ that leads us into ministry and service in the Church. But what are we to do when frustrations with the institutional Church, resistance to our pastoral presence, or outright aggression obstruct our fruitfulness in ministry? Is it sufficient to simply surrender our pain to Jesus in prayer? Will that always work? And if that doesn't work anymore, does that mean we don't pray hard enough?

How much pain can be transformed into redemptive suffering without crushing us altogether? And when does that pain become so debilitating that we need to get out before it kills our spirit? How do we discern when our pastoral presence is life-giving both to us and to the community of faith, and when it is time to shake the dust from our feet and go elsewhere? Is it even conceivable that God could lead us to other denominational pastures?

I have asked myself these questions many times, and continue to do so. My spiritual director – a wise and gentle priest – hears me voice them, especially at times of deep pain when I doubt myself, my vocation, my fruitfulness. At such times I end up asking God with great trepidation, Is it time to go – go from this place, this parish, these people, this Church even? How could I even contemplate leaving a tradition that is so deeply rooted in my self-identity? Sometimes my spiritual mentor simply lets me talk it through and I come to my own answers. Other times he says something like, "This hurts, yes. Just remember one thing: when you're ready, the God of the crucified and risen Jesus will teach you many things through this hurtful experience if you are open."

This mentor's unconditional regard for the validity of my experiences helps to keep me open and soft to God's touch instead of clamming up my spirit in bitterness and anger. Many times he simply leads me to Scripture, inviting me to connect my pain to specific moments in Jesus' life. This often has a healing effect and breaks the isolation that betrayals and injustices in the Church can cause. Other times he encourages me to set firm boundaries and to remove myself from an oppressive situation. The accountability and guidance that spiritual direction provides have proven to be crucial in order to keep such questions in their rightful context and to discern their source, motivation and purpose.

So far I have had an open window of opportunity to serve God's people in the Roman Catholic tradition, and I am deeply grateful for this. By and large, my ministry has been life-giving both to me and to the recipients of this ministry. I know, however, that my relationship with God in Jesus has to be front and centre, that this relationship is bigger than the Roman Catholic Church, and that my ministry in the Church derives its meaning and energy from that relationship, not the other way around. The divine–human partnership is dynamic in nature. Adding to this dynamic character is the fact that ministry roles for women in the Roman Catholic Church are not formally defined or recognized. This necessitates a dynamic relationship between the woman who feels called to ministry and the opportunities for ministry open to her at any given time. It should be no surprise that the shape and features of my response to God's call can change over time with changing circumstances.

A healthy detachment (such as that advocated by St. Ignatius[24]) and a healthy spirituality will not fear the hard questions, the pain and the possibility that someday other choices and decisions may need to be made. For most of us, the possibility of changing denominational affiliation may never need to be considered seriously. Some, however, have felt compelled, in response to God's call to serve in Christ's name, to allow their ministry to bear fruit in another Christian tradition.

8

Shaking off the Dust

Go from your country and your father's or mother's house
to the land that I will show you.

(Adapted from Genesis 12:1)

When God calls a person to a certain way of being in the world or in the Church, something comprehensive takes place inside the person. Call stories abound in the Scriptures – Moses, Isaiah, Jeremiah, Jesus and his disciples, Paul. Call stories also abound in the literature on saints and on holy people (Ignatius of Loyola, Francis of Assisi, Thomas Merton, Mother Teresa) and other, "non-church" folk, such as Albert Einstein, Florence Nightingale, or, in our day, Sheila Cassidy.[25] Besides these public lists, we each have a personal list of special people who model for us what it looks like to respond to God's call. For me, they include individuals like my own aunt who dared to marry a "foreigner"; friends who chose to be different; mentors in my years of studies; priests and lay people who take risks in the way they respond to God's stirrings in their hearts.

Contrary to popular opinion, however, God does not call extraordinary people. God calls each one of us to a fullness of life that finds expression through the unique features of our life situation, our gifts and our personality. A characteristic that authenticates a call as divine is its power to unleash in us a deep passion and to engage us in the depth and breadth of our being. The power of a divine call lies in its capacity to arouse the desire and the hope for a fullness of life that awaits us in our total response. We both fear and are attracted by a power that engages us so totally.

And so, when gifts were awakened that tapped my greatest potential and increased my desire to serve the Church, I naturally responded with both fear and yearning. And yet I understood rather quickly that such gifts and callings were not meant for personal sanctification or for another Christian tradition. Even though I heard God's call in the context of a Lutheran seminary within an ecumenical student body and faith community, this call did not come with any desire to change denominational allegiances. On the contrary, the ecumenical learning setting deepened my knowledge of, insights into and affection for my own Catholic heritage. However anxious, I trusted God's ability to allow my vocation to bear fruit in the Catholic community, even though there was no formal or automatic place for ministry exercised by a woman. But in terms of going elsewhere, there was no discussion.

As my ministry unfolded, however, I found myself regularly in sanctuaries and pulpits of other denominations. Preaching became the unexpected ecumenical ministry, and the fact that I was doing this as a non-ordained Catholic woman turned out to be in my favour. A Catholic priest remarked one day, "Protestant churches do not open their pulpits to a Catholic priest in the same way as they do to you. This is a great privilege, and clearly God's doing." In my capacity as supply preacher, I have the privilege and opportunity to be a bridge and a model for ecumenical dialogue. This is holy work that contributes to the spirit of unity for which Jesus prayed so fervently the night before he died.

But I would be lying if I denied that comments and invitations from those in other denominations never challenge my Catholic belonging – they do. Even though my current ecumenical preaching ministry bears clear features of God's imprint, the close association with non-Catholic denominations periodically does raise questions. After all, liturgical preaching – my greatest passion – in a Catholic context has become rare. Informal invitations to consider ordained ministry elsewhere continue to be a regular occurrence.

Discerning God's voice in such invitations requires ongoing prayer, honesty and vigilance of heart. Every time the question presents itself, I have been quick and clear with my response: I am part of the Body of Christ in the Catholic tradition and that is where God has planted me to bear fruit. As long as the window of opportunity to serve fruitfully in the Roman Catholic Church remains open, there is neither a need nor an attraction to go elsewhere. But is it possible that a day will come when my answer will change, or that my heart will no longer believe my own answer?

That day has come for some women. Their stories belong in this book because, in changing denominations, they have not left the Christian family of faith. Each woman contributed her story because she continues to cherish her deep Catholic roots in faith. In their eyes, the denominational discontinuity that they undertook was nevertheless a paradoxical expression of continuity in following Christ's call to discipleship.

*** BETTY ***

Betty and I meet in a quiet corner of a café on a sunny summer afternoon. After some small talk to get acquainted, she tells me her story.

Betty's maternal family was Roman Catholic, but her paternal family was Protestant (United Church of Canada). Although she was raised Roman Catholic and was deeply committed to this tradition, her ties with the other half of her church family were strong, too. This meant that, as a child, she would sometimes go to the Sunday services at the United Church, even though she knew it to be unacceptable according to the Catholic Church at that time. To resolve that dilemma, she would go to confession as soon as she could afterward.

When Betty was in Grade 2, she made a makeshift altar in her bedroom where she would "celebrate" Mass every morning. Her dolls and stuffed animals were the congregation. Toast or a cracker and juice were the Eucharistic elements. Her vestments included one of her mother's dresses, a scarf for a stole, and high-heeled shoes. She would recite the few Latin words that she could remember, and make up the rest in gibberish: "It was a holy time, deeply meaningful to my youthful imagination and desire," she says. One day, Betty told Sister at school what she was doing. Sister told her that she was being bad and displeasing to God, and that she'd better confess her sin: "I never 'celebrated' Mass again," Betty tells me, "but the dream remained in the recesses of my mind and heart."

*

With some sadness I think of my parents, who considered my religiosity "over the top" because I wanted to go to church more than once a week. I look away into the busy street, lost in thought for a moment. Betty notices and waits a while before she resumes.

*

In her mid-20s, Betty stopped going to church for about five years. She explains, "I recall feeling disillusioned, dry, and depressed about my life, my faith. I was 30 years old when I finally went to see my parish priest about how I was feeling." He listened attentively, and then invited her to come to a prayer meeting at the church. The Charismatic Renewal was in full swing at that time, and Betty was hooked. Scripture truly was the living Word. "Praise-filled singing lifted my spirit. Here I was being nourished and nurtured, and it gave me life. My heart opened up and I experienced the presence of the Holy Spirit in ways that astounded and gladdened me," she says.

The dry spell was over, and Betty resumed her involvement in the Church with more vigour and enthusiasm than before. Her gifts for ministry blossomed and were well received by the faith community. She participated as a liturgical reader and music leader, as a catechist for RCIA, in baptism and marriage preparation courses, and as a member of several diocesan commissions. Over the years, she attended numerous workshops, seminars, retreats and missions to develop her gifts for ministry and to satisfy her hunger for a deeper faith.

*

I nod fiercely in agreement. I cannot list all the workshops, retreats and seminars I have taken throughout the years. And I discovered that the more I learned, the hungrier I became for more. We both order another latte, knowing that we'll be here for a while.

*

During this time, Betty began to question some of the Church's teachings that she found difficult to accept. Among these were birth control, divorce, women's exclusion from church leadership, papal infallibility and institutional hierarchy. The all-male leadership in the Charismatic Renewal was a strong supporter of patriarchal hierarchy in the Church. Given her own increasing discomfort, it became clear to Betty that it was time to leave the Renewal in order to move forward in the direction in which she felt God was calling her.

In conversation with her parish priest, Betty agreed to wrestle with her concerns, to engage the struggle and to hope that she could continue to serve the Church. She was overjoyed when women were allowed to be Eucharistic ministers. "This helped to sustain me in the midst of the angst that I was experiencing, wondering if I truly belonged in the Roman Catholic Church when I was finding it so difficult to reconcile my beliefs and values with Rome's."

*

I do not share all of Betty's problems with church teaching. My husband and I have been certified teachers of Natural Family Planning with Serena Canada all our married life. We chose this not because of the Church's position on birth control, but much more so for environmental and health reasons. We find ourselves often silenced in a Church and in a culture that no longer values the witness of couples who choose effective alternative natural methods to regulate their families.

*

Betty was 49 years old when she went back to university to study. This course of action was prompted by a growing dissatisfaction with the ways her nursing career was taking her away from patients' bedsides into more administration, by a recognition of her desire to teach, and

by a sense of adventure. "Little did I know that my quest would lead
me to an Anglican seminary to study theology, where, after seven
years of study I would receive a Master of Divinity degree, followed
by a master's degree in Sacred Theology," she says. At the same time,
she embarked on her first unit of Clinical Pastoral Education (CPE
– hospital chaplaincy). The combination proved to be life changing.

*

My introduction to the Lutheran seminary, at age 36, was through a
similar program, called Pastoral Counseling Education (PCE). Little
did I know I would be there for seven years and then graduate with
a theology degree.

*

Although she was in the non-ordination stream at the seminary, the
courses Betty took were designed for students studying to become
Anglican priests. Her own Catholic bishop suggested a couple of
Catholic courses. By her second year, her fellow students were encouraging her to consider ordination. "They even presented me with
a red ordination stole," she says. "I was grateful for their support and
affirmation, but I wasn't ready to let go of my Catholic tradition."

Betty participated fully in the Anglican community at the seminary
and felt very comfortable doing so. She felt particularly blessed by
their liturgies and the inclusion of all at the Eucharistic table. She
recalls with particular fondness how exciting it was to see women
exercising their call to priesthood. On Sundays, she attended Mass
at a Catholic parish. Meanwhile, faculty and colleagues continued to
gently invite her to leave the door open to ordained ministry.

*

My non-Catholic fellow students offered feedback similar to the kind
Betty received. But in those years, changing denominations was never
a serious question for me, even though I became very puzzled as to
why God seemed to be calling me into something that was so diffi-

cult to realize in my Catholic tradition. Mary's question to the angel, "How can this be?" sprang from my heart.

*

After taking two basic units of Clinical Pastoral Education (CPE), Betty enrolled in a one-year residency in advanced CPE and a basic unit in Pastoral Counseling Education (PCE):

> We were an ecumenical group. One other woman and I were the only Roman Catholics. My experiences were rich and powerful. It was here that I began to discover and claim my own theology — not just what I had been taught to believe, but what I knew.

Through challenging experiences in which she was loved, accepted and respected, the truth of her being surfaced.

She discovered more of who she was both psychologically and theologically. Once this was brought into the light, she had much more energy for ministry as a chaplain. She continued in CPE, and was certified as a Spiritual Care Specialist. When she returned to the seminary after her CPE/PCE residency, she was much more grounded in her faith, in her sense of authority, and in her call to ordination. Still, the hour had not yet come: "I needed time to reflect, to talk, to grieve, to celebrate, to decide."

Following convocation for her Master of Divinity, Betty was hired part time as the associate chaplain at a long-term care facility. The Director of Spiritual Care was an ordained minister in the United Church of Canada. Betty thrived in ministry there, preparing and leading worship services, funerals and memorials, preaching and co-presiding at Holy Communion, teaching, and supervising spiritual care volunteers.

*

I marvel at God's gentle yet creative ways. As with Betty, God placed me in a pulpit to experience the preaching ministry. I discovered a gift, an unusual sense of belonging and a deep joy. "Another latte?" Betty asks. "No, thanks," I say.

*

Betty was subsequently hired by an Anglican parish as a part-time pastoral associate for an eight-month contract. Her ministry included pastoral education, preaching, pastoral visits and preparing memorial services. Shortly after being hired, Betty became a member of the Anglican Church, and entered a discernment process on the question of ordination. The selection committee discerned a call to orders, but Betty was not convinced that this was where God was calling her.

> I suppose some would say that I was being disobedient … But for me, it was paying attention to the still, small voice deep within me. I have learned to trust this place, and choose to wait and see. It was a liminal time, without knowing where this was leading. I had a strong sense that God was directing me, but where, what, when and how?

*

I think back on my first year after convocating with my theology degree. I had no job prospects, and was literally waiting on God to direct my steps. I knew that, as long as there was no clarity, there was no decision to be made about anything. And I waited, a full year, until the job came to me.

*

It was three months later, while holidaying with her best friend, that Betty's direction was revealed. "It was a *kairos* moment, and I knew without a doubt that I was called to ordained ministry in the United Church of Canada (UCC). This was the last place I would have thought of in my conscious mind!" Yet, in hindsight, it was obvious, as the UCC's ethos and theology had been a part of Betty's life all along. Following her holiday, God provided confirmation. Betty returned to work at the long-term care facility. Just as she was going into her office, a staff member approached her and asked her to consider applying for a part-time ministry position in her rural United Church congregation. "I was amazed," she says. "Two weeks later, I was hired by the congregation, and warmly received as an ex-Catholic/Anglican." In fact, she recalls that the people expressed the hope that she would bring her other Christian backgrounds to bear on her new ministry among them. After two years Betty joined the UCC, and is currently in a discernment process for ordination. She has not looked back.

*

After a full year of waiting after convocation, I was called forth in a surprising way. The superior of the Oblates of Mary Immaculate came to me with the following request: would I take on the editorship of the Canadian Catholic family magazine *Our Family*, published by the Oblates? I said yes, and remained in that position for nearly four years until the magazine was closed down. The editorship increased my writing confidence in preparation for becoming an author. I could never have planned this or known this ahead of time.

*

When I asked Betty about the most difficult challenge in her denominational transition, she recalls that moving from the Roman Catholic tradition to the Anglican tradition was gradual and relatively easy in terms of traditional similarities, but it was nevertheless painful: "My pain was caused by the sense of great loss: of a particular identity, of a particular faith community, of a particular kind of faith culture."

The other most difficult challenge now has been the absence of weekly Eucharist in the UCC. However, she is happy to report that this is changing, as people in the UCC are rediscovering the importance of and need for this sacrament in their lives. Having said this, Betty adds that by not having weekly Eucharist, she has developed a deeper love and appreciation for Scripture.

> In a very real way, this has been God's nourishment for my heart, mind and spirit. I am being sustained by God's graciousness in the Word, and at the same time I continue to long for and work for the day when Holy Communion will be celebrated alongside the Word in Sunday worship services. On that day, I shall feel complete.

*

I would have great difficulty giving up regular Eucharist, too. I don't know if I could ever change my denominational stripes. But my years with the Lutherans have resulted in a deep love for, and an intimate relationship to, the Scriptures, as Betty's years with the United Church have done for her. I will be forever grateful for this.

"How about a cool drink this time?" Betty asks. Sure. After all, it's summer, and we have to order again so we can legitimately take up a table.

*

In the United Church, Betty's gifts for ministry are supported and honoured as being equal to those of everyone else. She is able to live more truly who she is.

> I love the fact that the church is inclusive, cognizant of the dangers of patriarchy, open to diverse theologies, respectful of different faith traditions and cultures, and possessing a strong ministry of outreach and social justice. I, along with everyone else, have a voice in decision making – an important ethos if we are to hear what the Spirit is saying. I experience a deep joy in my ministry and feel at home.

Comparing her current ministry with the ministry she was allowed to exercise in the Catholic community, Betty observes that she now does ministry with a sense of authority that she did not have in the Roman Catholic tradition.

> It isn't a "power over" kind of authority, but rather an inner knowing that I have been called to this work and have been given the gifts, skills, experiences, education, support and affirmation of others to be an ordained minister in the UCC. I am free to live and become all that God has created me to be and do within a community of faith that does not put limitations on me because I am a woman.

Betty's love for the Eucharist encourages her to help her Protestant brothers and sisters to embrace this precious sacrament with more frequency. Her Anglican and Roman Catholic heritages encourage her to use ritual with candles and other symbols, musical instruments, dance, processions and banners as ways of creating sacred time and space in the liturgies. The gift she received from the Charismatic Renewal is spontaneity and joyful expression in worship of God, an expression that recognizes the presence of the Holy Spirit among and within all people.

> Now is a favourable time for me to be able to weave together aspects of my Catholic upbringing that have so blessed me. The UCC is recovering many meaningful traditions that were lost during and after the Reformation. In some ways, I feel that God is using me to help bring about reconciliation, to heal the brokenness that happened so long ago. At the same time, I am being healed by the UCC of the brokenness and rejection that I experienced as a Roman Catholic woman. God is so very compassionate, and so very gracious!

*

This is the surprising twist for me in Betty's story: that her catholicity has not disappeared from her life. In some sense, she has become a Catholic ambassador in the United Church. Smart thinking, God. "Can we have the bill now, please? My treat, Betty."

*

I asked Betty what she would say to other Catholic women who feel called to ministry.

> I'd simply share my experience of the importance of intentionally listening deeply to your own stories and to the stories of other women within both the Roman Catholic tradition and the Protestant tradition. Be as open and as trusting of God's Spirit as you can, and the Spirit will lead you to discover your truth – who you are, and who you are not. Look at how you have changed, at what you understand now that you didn't before.

> What are your passions and gifts, and how do you live them? Are you satisfied, happy? Reflect on meaningful life events, especially the unsettling surprises. Let yourselves feel your pain and sorrow, for they are your teachers, your wise ones who are working with you in discernment. Do not judge yourselves as wrong for thoughts and feelings that seem to be out of sync with what you

have been taught. Pay attention to your intuitions – your nudging, dreams and desires – and check them out with trustworthy others.

Above all, know that God is faithful, just, compassionate and patient, and will give you the grace to be the same. You will be brought to a place of blessing, peace and joy whatever your decision may be. May faith in the risen Christ be your inspiration, your power, and your wisdom.

*

We have been at the café far too long. But the encounter has done both of us good.

Betty's story confirms for me that, contrary to popular opinion, a denominational move is not considered lightly, nor is it done primarily out of spite or in anger. God calls without reserve, and without regard for denominational divisions and restrictions. Such divisions and restrictions are contrary to God's design and thus have their root in human sin. This becomes particularly painful for Catholic women who have a sense that they are called to ordained ministry. Some have lived with this knowledge for their entire lives.

A denominational move is akin to changing life partners and comes with the same complex set of issues and challenges. Such a decision is often made only after an agonizing process of soul-searching and discernment, one that involves intense and intimate confrontation with deep-seated Catholic understandings of revealed truth. A woman like Betty who enters such discernment finds herself wrestling within her own soul with many things: the real denominational differences in worship and theology, in ethos and practice, in the relationship between Scripture and tradition, to name but a few. On top of these real distinctions with Catholicism, she wrestles most notably with the Catholic refusal to recognize the Anglican and Protestant churches' ministerial ordinations and the refusal to acknowledge their celebrations of Eucharist as real and valid. The Catholic Church also questions these churches' understanding of the apostolic succession.

Moreover, such a woman faces the painful dilemma of reconciling the Church's prohibition on the ordination of women with her own experience of call. The discernment process can be very lonely, painful and complicated. It is often extremely difficult to accomplish without wise and steady accompaniment by seasoned mentors and a solid spiritual director.

*** SUSAN ***

I had talked with Susan, who is single and in her late 40s, on a number of occasions. Over supper in a restaurant, or sipping wine in her student room on campus, I had witnessed some of the agonizing process of denominational discernment in her. Susan decided to write out her contribution to my book, which she sent me on the eve of her ordination to the diaconate in the Anglican Church.

In a few days I am scheduled to be ordained as a deacon in the Anglican Church of Canada, with priestly ordination likely to follow within the year. Five years ago I never dreamed I would be in this position. I was a Roman Catholic woman until mid-life, and then moved, as my bishop worded it, from being a Catholic in the Roman tradition to being a Catholic in the Anglican tradition. In the "high" Anglican context, we kneel and cross ourselves often, dipping our fingers in the holy water of the baptismal font; and we use incense at major liturgies, reserve the consecrated elements in the tabernacle and observe most of the major Marian feasts.

I thought I knew Anglicanism quite well after spending decades in an ecumenical setting in which our Roman Catholic parish shared a building with Anglicans. I would attend their services at times, enjoying the poetic Elizabethan language of the *Book of Common Prayer* (BCP), the lovely old hymns played on organs, the married clergy with sermons based in family life, and the distinctly Canadian flavour of this relatively non-centralized church. I even loved the comparative poverty and smallness of many Anglican parishes, and far preferred them to today's Roman Catholic mega-parishes.

I loved their more flexible theology, in which Eucharist is both the real presence of Christ as well as a remembrance of Christ's Last Supper with his disciples and friends. I loved their open invitation to all baptized Christians to receive communion. I loved the rich opportunities that lay people had to exercise theological gifts (after suitable training), including preaching on Sundays and conducting funerals.

Meanwhile, Vatican II had taken place when I was in my teens, and it held out much hope for a fantastic new openness to the Spirit's gifts being allowed to flourish among so many people, some of whom were not celibate males. Since my early 20s I was convinced that women, too, were called to priesthood, since the soul has no gender. I met many women and married men whose gifts for ministry were strong, and so badly needed in the Church. I dedicated much time and energy to helping a Vatican II ecclesiology unfold over time. But as my 50th year approached, it became clear that the Roman retrenchment to pre-Vatican ways was not a passing fad. Moreover, many young conservatives seemed glad about that. They wanted to pull the plug, and "return" to a Church with far greater security and less ambiguity than the Vatican II model.

So I went to visit the Anglican bishop to speak of my lifelong attraction to a Church that was so similar to mine, with some notable exceptions, such as no pope, and no restrictions as to who is eligible to be considered for ordination. Through a flow of tears I told the Anglican bishop of the many issues in the Roman Catholic Church that I found appalling or deeply wounding. I had seen the Spirit stifled so many times, as gifted and educated people were set aside to do peripheral tasks, while Catholic bishops combed the corners of the globe for single, ordained males who might want to minister in Canada, but came from a culture whose values vastly differed from ours.

I had seen once too often my Protestant friends turned away from Catholic communion tables, and could not picture Jesus doing the same. I could no longer blink and look the other way at the way the sex abuse scandals were being handled, and Rome's continued insistence that any kind of sexual activity, even within heterosexual marriage, made you unsuited to be an ordained minister. The grief I bore at these and other issues in my Roman Catholic Church was getting beyond what I could still carry.

It was time to make the move. But I did not become Anglican in order to be ordained. In fact, it had been years since that old yearning had reared its hopeless head into my conscious psyche. That women were called, I knew with conviction, but my own sense of calling was buried deeply somewhere back in some trash heap of old discarded dreams and lost causes. And so, the bishop's question that day, "Do you think you might be called to Holy Orders?", took me completely by surprise!

After a while, I accepted the bishop's invitation to discern ordained ministry, and so began a challenging process of interviews, courses, internships and assessments, until finally, here I am, a few days away from being ordained. God chooses to be in partnership with fallen creatures – amazing. I know I am not truly worthy of this calling, because nobody can be. My sense of unworthiness, I was told, is an important part of my entry to ordained ministry. What a luxury, actually, to say and know that I am unworthy instead of always having to be defensive, to prove that women are equally worthy. Actually, it turns out that they are equally as unworthy as men are.

Here's another surprise: I experience very little "feminism" in the Anglican Church – there's no need, since gender is not a barrier. There is, of course, a compassionate concern about women's situations in many other places, including in the Roman Catholic Church, but this is not any kind of raging feminism. Amazing how calm people become when they do not have to prove that the Spirit dwells in them as much as it does in others. I wish Rome could see that if only women were treated like equals and true partners in ministry, they might not be so angry. It's a concept almost too simple to explain, and yet, apparently so difficult to comprehend. What blessed relief to be away from all that painful anger.

Since becoming Anglican I have met many deeply called and committed women clergy. I have prayed with them, cried with them, laughed with them, and served the poor beside them. In a few days, they will help the bishop lay hands on my head, in a succession that does indeed stretch back all the way to the first such events in the early Church. After that, a stole will be placed over my left shoulder, a stole magnificently made by a friend who is a single Anglican male seeking ordination, and has so far not been accepted for this path. I will pray that he, too, will find the open doors he needs to find, along with every other woman and man, married or not, whose gifts for ordained ministry cannot be ignored or suppressed much longer without peril to both their own sanity and to the well-being of the whole Christian Church, which is so badly in need today of the leadership these people could provide.

I am deeply touched by Susan's reflection. I also know at what cost this decision has come for her. Since her discernment (based in prayer, spiritual direction and an informed conscience) led her into another Christian tradition, she incurred automatic excommunication and henceforth is denied access to the Catholic sacraments. It is particularly painful to reconcile this excommunication with the fact that the gifts and call to ministry for women like Susan arose from the bosom of that same Church that called her to grow a mature faith in Jesus Christ. Her only consolations are the Catholic teaching on the supremacy of an informed conscience (to go against one's conscience violates one's inner being[26]), the strong Catholic commitment to Christian unity, the recognition that ecclesial divisions are a result of human sinfulness and not of divine design, and that Christ Jesus has not abandoned other churches because of the human-made rifts.

> In spite of [the differences] it remains true that all who have been justified by faith in baptism are incorporated into Christ ... many of the most significant elements and endowments which together go to build up and give life to the church itself, can exist outside the visible boundaries of the Catholic Church: the written Word of God; the life of grace; faith, hope and charity, with the other interior gifts of the holy Spirit, as well as visible elements. [...] separated churches and communities ... have been by no means deprived of significance and importance in the mystery of salvation. For the Spirit of Christ has not refrained from using them as means of salvation .... (*Decree on Ecumenism*, 3)

*** ELAINE ***

Like Betty, whose story is told earlier in this chapter, Elaine, a grandmother and widow, recalls that the seeds of her vocation were already present in early childhood. Elaine's Catholic formation and upbringing before Vatican II were based on doctrines, dogmas, biases, divisions, rigidities and even prejudices. Even as a young child Elaine knew someday she would need to forsake these. At age five, she asked her mother if she would always be in "this church." When her mother looked puzzled, Elaine explained that she just couldn't stay in a church that had only "dads" doing everything. ("What did I know at age 5?" she says.)

Her Celtic mother, who had been "broken in" by nine other children, sought to listen to Elaine's innocent heart rather than instill fear or guilt for even entertaining such a scandalous or sinful deviation. Elaine asked her if it was "bad" not to join in the prayer every Sunday in which God was asked to send "more dads / men" to join the priesthood: "Whatever her answer was, there was no condemnation. She asked why I didn't want to say that prayer. From the mouth of a babe I replied, 'Mom, I am supposed to be doing what those dads are doing.'" Her mother did not squelch or judge Elaine's childhood fantasy – or was it God-given wisdom, vision or prophecy? The year was 1940. The Depression had just come to an end.

Like a seed, this "knowing" remained with Elaine, but it would only blossom much later, in God's time. Fast-forward eleven years: it was 1951 in Grade 11 at an all-girls' boarding school. The bishop addressed the grade 11 and 12 students. He spoke of the refusal of young men to accept their call to the priesthood. He rhetorically asked if the girls and their families were praying for their brothers or other boys to become priests, and predicted that when the girls were finished school, married and raising families (what else was there for girls to do?), there would not be enough priests to have daily Mass.

Elaine had six older brothers, none of whom was considering priesthood. She felt the "guilt" being placed on her shoulders. Elaine recalls glancing towards the back of the room where Mother Superior and Sister Mary Janet, school principal, were sitting. She saw Mother Superior close her eyes and put her hand to her throat. "Was she praying for laryngitis ... for me? The message I internalized was: Elaine, be quiet!"

Then, Sister Mary Janet walked up to Elaine's desk – in the front row, of course – and gently touched her arm. Was this another message? Yes, Elaine thought, so she spoke up to the bishop.

> Bishop, our family prays. Our town has a Pentecostal Bible School and they all pray, too. I believe God answers prayer and I think God is answering our prayer for vocations but that we don't understand it.

Approaching her desk, the bishop asked Elaine what that answer might be. Elaine replied, "I believe in 20 years the people in this room [remember, an it was an all-girls' boarding school in 1951] will be doing what priests and bishops are doing today." Silence followed.

A resounding gasp came from the back desk. Classmates waited for a response.

The bishop went to the window and looked out. He then came to Elaine and looked deeply into her eyes, into her very soul.

> I felt vulnerable and exposed and naked. I waited. He reached out his hands and grasped mine and he said, "I probably won't be alive in 20 years, but you will be. If you are being called (he stopped before saying "to the priesthood"), promise me you will answer." Then he said, "Class dismissed."

Only after raising her own family, and the untimely death of her husband, did Elaine recover these tiny seeds from her past, and the old desire to serve in ministry returned to her heart. She pursued an impressive course of studies, and eventually was hired as a pastoral associate in a large urban parish by a priest who had also been a friend for many years. She was responsible for adult education, sacramental formation and liturgy. Things looked promising. Her ministry was well received until jealousy, cowardice and betrayal started to poison the workplace. "Confusion set in," she recalls. "Communication lacked honesty when I sought clarity." She remembers a parishioner taking her aside and warning her to "watch her back."

Still, she was convinced that her honesty and integrity could stifle the immature and cowardly backstabbing that had started to infect her ministerial contributions in the parish. After a doctor-ordered stress leave, she faced the final result.

> The day before I was to return to "active duty," I was summoned to a meeting by the administrator and a woman lawyer who was council chairperson. I asked why the priest was not at the meeting. I was told that my legal dismissal had nothing to do with him. And, indeed, it was a legal document, wrapped in lawyer's jargon and iron-clad conditions. New keys for the office had been cut. I was to clear out my office.

Elaine's world fell apart. She journalled and journalled – pages and pages, books and books. She let the words flow and the tears spill everywhere.

I did not suppress any thoughts or feelings. I cried out to God, I shouted at God. Yes, I think I even cursed the day I was born. Then, I read and re-read these holy and inspired journal writings and listened … as my Mother had listened to me … to what they were teaching me, to what the Spirit was saying.

She felt like a wandering nomad without a home. She felt as if she had been robbed of her birthright. She went to other Catholic churches where she became a nameless spectator, without a welcome, without a smile. The perfunctory handshake presupposing "peace" seemed to be transmitted in some sort of soulless fashion. Her long-standing Sunday practice of gathering to celebrate Eucharist was shaken. Her heart yearned to see, touch and be Jesus, in and through community, but for Elaine the Roman Catholic ritual of Eucharist now seemed empty, devoid of sanctifying grace.

For nine months she asked herself:

"What was my time? What season was I in?" Every day I looked out my patio window onto the park. Trees burst forth with life and greenness. Leaves whistled and whispered in the wind. They turned golden, they dried up and fell to the ground. Branches became barren. Yet, I believed, I had to believe, that there was life and hope in that sterile trunk.

I am gripped by Elaine's story – this all sounds way too familiar. She continues,

Each Monday, I promised myself, if I wasn't better by next Monday, I would go and see a psychiatrist. The first, second and third "trimester" came and went … and one day I tasted the divine. God was around me, behind and in front of me and in me. The dark night of the soul had lifted and I was indeed a new creation.

She had reached a fork in the road. It was decision-making time, discernment time. The intensity of her emotions and physical pain had disturbed her everyday life for nearly a year, and seemed as if they had destroyed her life. Who was she? Where did she belong? Where could she find a spiritual home? Where was God in all of this?

She sought out other sacramental churches: Lutheran and Anglican. One Sunday she attended a United Church. The minister greeted her and called her by name. He remembered her from the few ministerial meetings she had attended. He said, "I have heard that horrible things have happened to you; is that true?" She nodded feebly. He said, "We welcome you to worship with us."

A few weeks later he asked her to drop by. He said, "Elaine, you have too many talents and gifts not to be using them. How would you like to minister here?" Elaine told him to ignore her for three or four months and just let her "be" and "become." Meanwhile, the congregation extended hospitality and friendship to her. After several months, the pastor felt it was her time, and Elaine knew it.

> I began ministering with retreats, workshops, spiritual direction, leading worship in a seniors' residence, membership on the liturgy board, and eventually preaching and leading Sunday worship for the pastor's summer holidays and during the Christmas season. People made me feel I belonged. I felt I belonged. My Catholic background was most appreciated. Women were accepted in full ministry, communion was for everyone – "Say but the word and I will be healed." Sex did not colour or dominate the church's ethos. I fit. Home at last!

Then Elaine, now well into her 60s, recalled what she had felt and said to her mother when she was five years old,

> and what I had felt and said to the bishop and what he had said to me. I again felt holy hands tenderly caressing my hands. I felt eyes enmeshed with my soul. I recalled the words "I probably won't be alive in 20 years, but you will be. If you are being called, promise me you will answer." And I "re-membered" myself – mind, heart, soul and body united, and I was whole. I was peaceful and happy.

> I knew that what had happened previously had been allowed for a reason. Life can make us better or bitter. The pain and struggle, God's grace and openness of heart, were making me better, not than anyone else, but better than I was. I was and continue to be very grateful for my Roman Catholic upbringing. Now my Catholicism is not denominational but truly universal: "I believe in one, holy, catholic/universal church...."

I wept and wept on that quiet fall afternoon in Elaine's living room as I was passing through on a weekend visit. There were painful connections, as I too had lived through a very hurtful parish dismissal. I wept because of the profound sense of loss from such a betrayal: the loss of trust and truth, the loss to the Catholic Church of gifted women like Elaine, the loss of parish integrity. I kept wondering whether going elsewhere is the only solution.

It may be bittersweet, but the surprise and consolation that awaits many women like Elaine is that, once they serve in another denomination, their Catholic heritage is not only appreciated but often actively called forth by the congregation and tradition they serve, and it becomes part of their attempts to work toward Christian unity. Though they are formally cast out by Rome, and though their decision to "leave" often incurs misunderstanding and criticism from fellow Catholics, such women can become ecumenical catalysts and role models on the other side of the ecclesial divide. Indeed, God can and will use anything and anyone to gather all people into one family:

> For as the rain and the snow come down from heaven, and do not return there until they have watered the earth, making it bring forth and sprout, giving seed to the sower and bread to the eater, so shall my word be that goes out from my mouth; it shall not return to me empty, but it shall accomplish that which I purpose, and succeed in the thing for which I sent it. (Isaiah 55:10-11)

*** ANNE ***

For some women, a call to ministry (ordained and otherwise) is initially lived out as a call to religious life. This was the case for Anne, who was a Carmelite nun for twelve years.

When I ring her doorbell, it takes a long time before the door is opened. It turns out that Anne is still recovering from a serious car accident and she walks with great difficulty. She settles down in her comfortable chair and directs me to the tea-making in the kitchen. Once we are both sipping the hot, aromatic brew, she begins. She knows why I have come; I want to hear her story of call and of denominational transfer.

She recalls the onset of the transition time in her life. In one year, she had experienced three major crises in her life involving the death of all the other women in her family. During the time her sister was dying, Anne met an Anglican priest who pastorally cared for her and took her to an Anglican Eucharist. To her surprise, Anne discovered that Anglican liturgy was not much different from the Roman Catholic Mass. This Anglican priest asked her one day, "What do you want to be doing five years from now?" Anne continues,

> I realized I did not want to be a Carmelite nun, nor did I want to be in the Roman Catholic Church. I decided to discern if this was what God was call- ing me to be, so I took a year's leave of absence and enrolled in a full year training program for Clinical Pastoral Education (CPE). I received all sorts of confirmation during the program and decided I would try to be admitted to a seminary, and I was. Doors kept opening to me year after year, and before I knew it, I was ordained.

> The most difficult aspect of the denominational transition was friends who asked, "Why have you left the Church?" I would try to explain that I had not left the *catholic church* (lower case) only the *Roman* Catholic Church. I found the Anglican Church to contain all I believe and none of what I didn't believe. I had a love of the sacraments and they were very much there. All in all, I had a very easy transition to the Anglican Church. The most rewarding part of this ministry has been the ability to celebrate the sacraments and to bring them to people in times of crisis or need. It has also been rewarding, although challenging, to preach.

> In many ways my ministry is now very, very different. I was a nun for my last twelve years as a Roman Catholic. I have now been rector of a number of churches, am able to celebrate and to administer the sacraments and be in- volved in people's lives in a tangible way. As a Carmelite we prayed for people, which was important also, but not the same. I feel I bring much of the Catholic spirituality with me, and this enriches my Anglicanism. In reality, I bring most of my Roman Catholic heritage with me, except for the authority structure and the top-down decision making, and I don't miss these. I revel in a church that finds its authority in God's people and in the local ordinary, the bishop.

> If a Catholic woman feels called to ministry, the first thing is to begin a careful discernment process with those you trust, with the faith community to which

you feel called and with the wider church of that denomination. I wish I could believe that change will happen in the Roman Catholic Church, but I don't. If one feels strongly called from God, it probably will not go away.

*

Hearing the stories of these four women affirms what I already feared: choosing ordination in another Christian tradition is not necessarily the easier route. The dilemma forced upon such women to choose between their beloved Catholic tradition, which encouraged them to grow a mature faith, and their calling from God, which that same tradition does not recognize, creates a most painful crucible. Asked whether she had found peace, one woman replied,

> My decision is very bittersweet. Yes, I feel free. I no longer have to get upset, because now I am allowed to be who I am. But I have paid a very high price. I love the Roman Church with my whole heart and soul. I never wanted to leave it. I sobbed for at least five years. I truly celebrated my leap of faith on the day of my ordination and I know it was the right thing to do. But that doesn't make it easy.

> It can be very lonely on this side of the ecclesial divide. But, what a blessing this present faith community is to me. By the end of a week, the feelings of grief about leaving gang up on me. But then I get to stand at the altar and in the middle aisle to proclaim the Gospel and celebrate the Eucharist, and I am uplifted again. God has blessed me with this experience to sustain me, I know. I had no choice but to leave. It was killing me to stay. I do feel more alive now. And it hurts a lot. I think it's called the cross. We women are carrying a very heavy cross right now, whether we leave or stay. My choice was both a cross and a resurrection. Bittersweet indeed.

9

The Cloud of Witnesses

Therefore, since we are surrounded by so great a cloud of witnesses, let us also lay aside every weight and the sin that clings so closely, and let us run with perseverance the race that is set before us, looking to Jesus the pioneer and perfecter of our faith, who for the sake of the joy that was set before him endured the cross, disregarding its shame, and has taken his seat at the right hand of the throne of God.

(Hebrews 12:1-2)

Dear Sarah,

It has been nearly three years since the day I heard you preach at your Grandpa's funeral vigil. Now 22 years old, you are away at university, diligently studying as well as offering your gifts of music and ministry at the local parish. It was your call to ministry, Sarah, so tangible the evening of the vigil, that motivated me to write this book. I realize with a new urgency that our lives do not belong to us, but are God's gift to God's people. It struck me again the evening of your Grandpa's vigil that we are connected in Christ Jesus, and that you and your contemporaries need help, guideposts and encouragement on this arduous yet so fulfilling journey with God and with the Church.

But now that you've read about our mixed experiences of joy and sorrow you must wonder: are they nuts?! It probably did not take you long to figure out that our callings and ministries clearly place us "between worlds." We live out our baptismal calling, yet we also claim a specific ministerial calling. This ministerial calling is expressed in a variety of concrete forms and places of service in the Church, yet for the most part this calling does not receive much of a formal man-

date, protection or blessing from that Church. We are leaders of communities, yet yield to the ordained pastor. We comfort and guide, teach and preach, yet we often do this without institutional affirmation. Many of us match ordained presbyters in theological and pastoral formation, yet our jobs are never guaranteed. The Church needs us, yet is ambivalent about us.

Knowing of God's call burning in your heart, Sarah, and writing to you, makes me feel a bit like St. Paul when he wrote to his dear young friend Timothy, whom he regarded as an adopted son, his protegé. Should you get lost or discouraged, I want to echo to you, Sarah, St. Paul's advice to young Timothy: remember who and whose you are, rekindle the faith, do not be ashamed, join your suffering to Christ, rest in God's grace, and hold fast to sound teaching (Timothy 1:6-11).

Also remember that once you've kissed the pearl of great price in your heart, your vocation to which God is calling you, there is nothing you cannot endure. You are in good company. As you said in a recent e-mail to me when you acknowledged your uncertain future, "Even if you can only see as far as your headlights, you can make the whole trip that way." Do not get discouraged if you only see the headlights most of the time. And living in-between times is very biblical!

At the close of this book, I hope that you realize not everything has been said here. Quite the contrary: our stories are merely the opening movement to a brand-new symphony that is being written with the lives of all women in the church. You and your contemporaries will write the next score with your own lives in service to the Gospel of Jesus.

In closing, we women of God, past-present-future, offer you a chorus of voices to sustain you on the way. Each of us looks to others for inspiration, guidance and encouragement. These voices come from strong women of faith, foremothers, saints, sisters and role models, past and present. Our list includes formal and informal saints, public and personal saints. They have all known the joy and ecstasy of knowing Jesus intimately and of offering their very lives in sacrifice and love to the living Body of Christ, our beloved Catholic Church. Together we are your shoulders, your cheerleaders in Christ Jesus our Lord.

Marie-Louise

*** FROM YOUR SISTERS IN MINISTRY ***

My soul magnifies the Lord,
and my spirit rejoices in God my Saviour,
for he has looked with favour on the lowliness of his servant.
Surely, from now on all generations will call me blessed;
for the Mighty One has done great things for me,
and holy is his name. (Luke 1:47-49)

Betty – My most significant role models have been other women I have met who exhibit qualities I admire. These women inspire me to be both coura-geous and charitable in my pastoral ministry: not to downplay my strengths, but to be patient with the time it takes for people to grow, and to empower and nurture others with the strength of a mother who encourages and cares for her children.

His mercy is for those who fear him
from generation to generation.
He has shown strength with his arm;
he has scattered the proud in the thoughts of their hearts.
He has brought down the powerful from their thrones,
and lifted up the lowly;
he has filled the hungry with good things,
and sent the rich away empty. (Luke 1:50-53)

Carla – A Jesuit priest friend has been a significant role model, as he defines his ministry by who he is as a person in relation to Christ, rather than drawing his authority from his ordination. And an elderly priest, who died two years ago, taught me to remember that the rules we create as a Church should be applied in pastoral situations only if they are about helping people know that God loves them. His grave is in the cemetery down the street from my house, and I visit his grave to pray with him whenever I need his inspiration.

He has helped his servant Israel,
in remembrance of his mercy,
according to the promise he made to our ancestors,
to Abraham and to his descendants forever. (Luke 1:54-55)

Darlene – The life of Mary Ward (1585–1645 – foundress of the Institute of the Blessed Virgin Mary [IBVM], a religious order for women) was an intimate part of my formation during high school and the early years of my religious life. She followed an Ignatian spirituality. Her life journey was difficult, but she built on unshakeable faith in God during decades of persecution of Catholics in England. She kept her eyes steadfastly on one thing – the will of God – and bent her entire resolve to following God's will as it was made known to her. She entered an order of Poor Clares on the continent, left them and founded an English-speaking order of Poor Clares that still exists today. Ultimately, she left them and founded the IBVM. She experienced persecution from within the Church, but persevered with faith and courage. Today, her order is worldwide. Mary Ward is a great inspiration for me.

Teresa of Avila is a guide for the heights, those moments on the mount of unitive embrace; for the lowlands, when we wonder if we can ever climb up again; for the plateaus, when we would just as soon get up a tent and stop moving. In every situation, positive or negative, Teresa is with us urging us to see where we are as simply another starting point for further journeying inward to God.[27]

Audrey – When it comes to church ministry, perhaps my greatest role model was my father. I think it was his love for liturgy that first influenced me. I remember going to "high Mass" with him in the 1950s. Another role model is my best friend, Leslie. She was a religious educator and then a pastoral associate in a parish on the west coast. I have called her many times for advice and assistance. Then there are a number of my priest friends with whom I studied theology. They are all remarkably "non-clerical" and believe in the "full, conscious, active participation" of all God's people. Probably my greatest role model is a good friend and mentor, Fr. Bob. Bob is passionate about music and liturgy, passionate about his priesthood and about lay ministry, passionate in his love for God. He has certainly fuelled my passion for music, liturgy and ministry.

Wylma – Teresa of Calcutta left the Loretto Sisters (another name for the IBVM Sisters) to found the Missionaries of Charity. Mary Ward's charism, and that of her order, was faith. Teresa's charism, and that of her order, was love. Darlene and I were also called to leave the Loretto Sisters, to live and work among First Nations people and to be able to invite others to do so. The charism granted to us is one of hope and healing. Teresa is an inspiration to me because she, like Mary Ward, followed God's call to her fullest ability.

There is no such difference between men and women that women may not do great things, as we have seen by the example of many saints. And I hope to God it will be seen that women in time to come will do much ... If women were made so inferior to men in all things, why were they not exempted in all things as they are in some? ... As if we were in all things inferior to some other being which I suppose to be a man! Which I dare be bold to say is a lie; and with respect to the good Father may say it is an error.[28] — *Mary Ward*

Gladys – Thérèse Arcand, a First Nations woman, was a Grey Nun who served during the 1970s. She made an effort to begin a religious order for aboriginal women. Two or three interested young women lived with her as postulants. Her efforts did not have the result she strove for. One of the young women subsequently joined the Grey Nuns. Thérèse inspires me because she was faithful to God's call as she discerned it and did what was open to her in her situation at the time in order to follow God's inspiration and respond to a clear practical need. There was a pervasive conviction in Canada that lasted well into the 1970s that native people "didn't have vocations." At the same time across the country, there was already a scarcity of vocations, both priests and religious, to serve First Nations church communities. To this day, more and more of these communities have been virtually abandoned. At the same time, little has been done to enable Native people to follow such vocations when they perceive that God is calling them to serve the Church. Thérèse Arcand remains an inspiration to me because she was a visionary; seeing the signs of the times, she took what action was open to her.

To me the will of God is a dear book which I am never tired of reading, which has always some new charm for me ... I cannot tell you what a beautiful thing the will of God seems to me. ... [At times] I was so weary of the struggle, and felt so utterly alone, could not pray or say my ordinary rosaries, only offered my weary heart's trials to my God ....[29]— *Mary MacKillop*

Sharon – Initially, most significant for me was a parish priest who accepted me unconditionally and who challenged me to grow. I had given up on life ever having anything significant in store for me; he gave me new hope. He challenged me to grow, supporting me in my struggles. He is the kind of friend who is not much for writing or phoning, but I know that, to this day, if I needed help, he would drop everything and come.

Arlene – I have two significant role models. One is a sister in my own former religious community and the other is my spiritual director. They love, support and challenge me not to grow complacent on my inner and outer journey with Christ. Both have great integrity and compassion and I would be happy to be considered to be like them.

I feel the vocation of the warrior, the priest, the apostle, the doctor, the martyr. Finally, I feel the need and the desire of carrying out the most heroic deed for You, O Jesus … I feel in me the vocation of the priest. With what love, O Jesus, I would carry You in my hands when, at my voice, You would come down from heaven. And with what love would I give you to souls![30]— *Thérèse of Lisieux*

Deanna – Kateri Tekakwitha (1656–1680) is a much beloved saint among Aboriginal people. Not much known in western and northern Canada, she lived a life of extraordinary hardship and love. Kateri met some nuns on her travels; she hoped to start a convent for Native women in Sault St. Louis but her spiritual director, Father Pierre Cholonec, discouraged her (or would not allow her to do so?). Kateri inspires me because her love for God was so total; she spent herself on prayer and on practical service to those around her, caring for the sick, teaching about Jesus by word and example.

Marlene – A former priest (now married with a family) was instrumental in allowing me to see how God loves, and how we can respond in love. To this day, I call on his example for many things and have adopted many of his attitudes in ministry. Other priests have been significant role models, particularly some who were my professors. They have modelled openness and ecumenical, interfaith attitudes that I totally embrace.

Arlene – Women within and outside the Roman Catholic Church have given me strength at times when I thought I had none left. While no particular mentor or role model comes to mind, there are many who have providentially entered my life during the past years of my ministry.

Anne – I met an Anglican priest while my sister was dying. She pastorally cared for me and took me to an Anglican Eucharist. She has been a mentor for me, and a role model for my own priestly ministry, over the last 18 years.

Sometimes, as we look at the night sky, a single bright star will appear. In its brightness it transforms the night; every star in the sky is changed in relation to this new appearance. It is as if this one star, in unparalleled beauty, crowns the entire beauty of the night. Christ in God is like that bright star, illumining the actuality of the primordial nature through the beauty of his manifestation of that nature in our history. Through Christ the depths of God are touched for the world; new possibilities for reflecting divine harmony in human history shine out for us. The church is born.[31]— *Marjorie Hewitt Suchocki*

Wylma – Mary Anne (1914–2002), my mother, and Mary (1913–2002), my co-worker's mother, were both women of great faith, perseverance and practical love. They shared their faith whenever and wherever possible. They were businesswomen and highly practical. They taught their daughters the knowledge and love of God from early childhood, as well as a range of skills for whatever life might bring. Our mothers are a very real and daily inspiration.

Francine – I identify very strongly with the Mary Magdalene of the Gnostic Gospel of Mary. She was called by Jesus, accompanied him, and was commissioned by him to spread the Gospel. She had a unique relationship with him, and he taught her things that the others just didn't get. She had friends, followers and supporters. She also had those who resented her for those very reasons. I see her as intelligent, wise and courageous. I may not have all the same attributes, but it is with that image and model that I identify most strongly.

Every cycle has its prophets – as guiding stars; and they are the burning candles of the Lord to light the spiritual temple on earth, for the time being. When they have done their work, they will pass away, but the candlesticks will remain, and other lights will be placed in them.[32] — *Antoinette Doolittle*

Darlene – When the Loretto Sisters first sent my partner and me into missionary work, we went through some very trying months of discernment and waiting. The greatest encouragement and support came from "the old sisters" in the religious community. They were in their late seventies, and in their eighties; they understood more than anyone what we were being called to and what it would mean for us to follow that call. They encouraged us to wholehearted giving without looking back. They themselves had lived in pioneer hardship in the early years in Saskatchewan and in rural Ontario. They had lived with few material goods, dependent on gifts in kind from those they served, who were themselves poor. They had started new ventures and followed new visions. They understood without needing explanations. They were eager for the order to send us out where we might be most needed. The thought of their encouragement still warms my heart.

Marlene – Jean de Brébeuf was an important figure in my childhood years. I read his accounts in the Jesuit Relations and saw his zeal, perseverance and courage as a model to be followed.

Annette – My mother was a woman of the Church in the fullest sense. She trained a choir in a new rural mission parish, taught the parishioners about the Mass, visited the sick, taught young mothers, took seminarians to task for language and behaviour when they came on holiday, and took in hand the various visiting priests as well as the pastor, letting them know when their sermons did not reach the people. For this service in her diocese, she received a papal medal *Pro Ecclesia et Pontifice.* Her comment: "I found it easier to deal with priests before Vatican II. Then they listened to me far more!"

A new year at the hand of the Lord Jesus – we do not know whether we shall experience the end of this year. But if we drink from the fount of the Saviour each day, then each day will lead us deeper into eternal life and prepare us to throw off the burdens of this life easily and cheerfully at some time when the call of the Lord sounds. ... God is my light and my salvation – of whom shall I be afraid?[33]— *Edith Stein*

Lenora – I identify strongly with the women mentioned in the Gospel of Luke: "Soon afterwards [Jesus] went on through cities and villages, proclaiming and bringing the good news of the kingdom of God. The twelve were with him, as well as some women who had been cured of evil spirits and infirmities: Mary, called Magdalene, from whom seven demons had gone out, and Joanna, the wife of Herod's steward Chuza, and Susanna, and many others, who provided for them out of their resources" (Luke 8:1-3).

My faith in Jesus has brought about so much healing in my life; it is a gift to be able to offer my gratitude in pastoral ministry to the Church. Like the women mentioned by Luke, I too provide service to God in the Church out of my personal resources.

Betty – I have always deeply respected my grandmother, who lived a life totally devoted to the Church. She in turn passed this on to my mother, who had all of us children extremely involved in the Church from a very young age.

Elaine – My grandfather's three sisters were Benedictine nuns, and we had two very close family friends who are Oblate priests. So I grew up with people in the house visiting who were living out their vocations to religious life. I am sure that this has affected my view of my own vocation.

Millie – Mary Ward is the foundress of the order to which I belonged for 20 years. On her tombstone it is written: "To love the poor, persevere in the same, live, die and rise with them was all the aim of Mary Ward." She was a seventeenth-century laywoman of courage and daring, an indomitable woman who persevered in her call to serve in the Church in spite of misunderstanding, imprisonment by church authorities, persecution by civil authorities, difficulties in dealing with both religious and secular clergy, and the inevitable difficulties with church authority because she was "just a woman."

Considering the mystical body of the Church, I had not recognized myself in any of the members ... or rather I desired to see myself in them all. Charity gave me the key to my vocation. I understood that if the Church had a body composed of different members, the most necessary and most noble of all could not be lacking to it, and so I understood that the Church had a heart and that this heart was burning with love. I understood it was Love alone that made the Church's members act, that if Love ever became extinct, apostles would not preach the Gospel and martyrs would not shed their blood. I understood that Love comprised all vocations, that love was everything, that it embraced all times and places ... In a word, that it was eternal. Then, in the excess of my delirious joy, I cried out: O Jesus, my Love ... my vocation, at last I have found it ... my vocation is Love![34] — *Thérèse of Lisieux*

Francine – I have in my office a collection of butterflies. I always feel that if people (myself included) are treated with respect and are given the right conditions, they can become something or someone they could not imagine.

Also, it is a reminder that we need to look at the potential of a person and what is on the inside. Who would ever imagine that a little caterpillar could ever turn into a beautiful butterfly?

Audrey – Mary Magdalene is my model in ministry and my inspiration. Even though legend does her a grave injustice by focusing on her questionable past, she is a powerful witness to the newness of life that God's forgiveness in Jesus brings. It was to her that the risen Christ first appeared; he called and commissioned her first: "Go and tell ...." As I minister to my people, bringing Christ's love through the quality of my presence, Mary Magdalene walks with me, and together we bathe in resurrection light, covering the earth with our joy and laughter. "We have seen the Lord!"

Certainly when I lie in jail thinking of these things, thinking of war and peace, and the problems of human freedom ... and the apathy of great masses of people who believe that nothing can be done, I am all the more confirmed in my faith in the little way of St. Thérèse. We do the minute things that come to hand, we pray our prayers, and beg also for an increase of faith – and God will do the rest.[35]— *Dorothy Day*

Carla – I see uncanny resemblances between St. Catherine of Siena and today's women in ministry. Catherine's ministry of preaching, negotiation, service, correspondence, mediation and admonishment of popes, laity and priests was unparalleled for a woman in her time, and derived its authority unequivocally from her conviction that God called her to speak and write. Today's women in ministry are motivated by the profound experience of God calling them. We are there for no other reason. Often we have no job security or good pay, we have to finance our own theological and pastoral education, and there is no guarantee that the Church will employ us. Yet like Catherine, we are driven to respond to the voice of love in our hearts. That voice nudges us into places of ministry heretofore restricted to ordained presbyters. Like Catherine, we hold no authority or office in the Church, and our gifts are more often viewed with suspicion than welcomed with enthusiasm and respect. Like Catherine, we root ourselves deeply in prayer, in the sacraments and spiritual nourishment of various kinds in order to feed our courage and faithfulness to Christ who calls us. Together with Catherine, the conviction that God's Spirit propels our speech, our service, our presence in ministry, sustains us even in the face of being ignored or dismissed.

Sharon – I had a teacher in Grade 6 whose memory to this day is an inspiration. She was not only an excellent teacher, but she radiated simplicity and joy. She affirmed and encouraged even when I had trouble learning something. She was faithful and virtuous, and modelled that in both word and deed. She had the gift of putting me at ease and encouraging me to reach higher, to try again, to trust, to take risks, to fear not the new and untried. I always hoped that I could become like her.

A soul rises up, restless with tremendous desire for God's honour and the salvation of souls. She has for some time exercised herself in virtue and has become accustomed to dwelling in the cell of self-knowledge in order to know better God's goodness toward her, since upon knowledge follows love. … [By] prayer the soul is united with God, following in the footsteps of Christ crucified, and through desire and affection and the union of love he makes of her another himself.[36]— *Catherine of Siena*

Marie-Louise – Professors at the theology department were a real inspiration. They affirmed and challenged me to explore ever-wider horizons, both within myself and within the Church. I discovered gifts, dreams and callings I never knew existed. One woman professor in particular, who was an ordained Protestant pastor, modelled a depth of ministry in liturgy and pastoral presence that touched me deeply. Her witness continues to be a source of hope and courage for my own ministry in the Catholic community.

Gladys – Several priests have been instrumental in my faith development. They used to come and have dinner at our family table when I was still a child. I remember lively conversations with my parents and the priest, in a pervasive light of joy and respect, even when they disagreed. I am fortunate to still have good priests in my current circle of support.

Anne – My mother has been the greatest role model in my life. Mom was practical, blunt, creative, and a woman who wove great faith into her daily life. Her ministry as a woman in a small, rural Irish Catholic parish was limited to teaching religion to the younger children, doing the linen (because we were the only ones in the parish with an iron!), lots of church cleaning, cooking for parish socials and anything else that came up. But Mom's real ministry was in her devotion to her prayers for everyone and everything, offered through many family rosaries as well as her morning prayers after breakfast, seated in her favourite chair amidst the chaos of a large family. She reached out to the sick in the town and to those mourning the loss of a loved one. Mom's funeral was huge, filled with people who shared how she had been there for them, and they were honoured to return the favour. Now I am proud when family members and old friends tell me, "You're just like your mother," something I tried to deny when I was younger!

Margaret Anna Cusack was born May 6, 1829, in Dublin, Ireland. A strict Anglican, Margaret Anna eventually entered an Anglican convent. Influenced by the Oxford Movement, she converted to Catholicism in 1858, and entered a Poor Clare community in Ireland. She dedicated herself to writing, especially on behalf of the liberation of women and children who were victims of oppression in Church and society. ... She founded the Sisters of St. Joseph of Peace and went to the USA to help young Irish girls arriving there. Conflict with the Archbishop of New York led other bishops to reject the new community. In 1888 she returned to England. ... Abandoned by the Roman Catholic Church, she died with the blessing of the Anglican Church and was buried in Leamington cemetery.[37]

Millie – I have had many excellent role models: my parents, a young priest in my youth, etc. For now, Mother Teresa stands out. When faced with a difficult situation, I try to think what she would do.

Deanna – I would have to say that the priest with whom I worked in my previous job has been, and still is, a significant role model for me. We have known each other for almost 20 years. He encouraged me to study. He is a great believer in adult education in the faith. A marvellous teacher, he has taught theology in the diocesan lay formation program for many years. He teaches with authority and awakens a desire in his students to learn even more. He is largely responsible for calling forth gifts that I never knew I possessed. In addition, he has encouraged me to continue my studies. Now that I work in prison ministry, I can still call on him for friendship and advice.

Marie-Louise – An Orthodox priest was my spiritual director for several years. It didn't matter what questions, fears or struggles I brought to our conversations: he modelled God's unconditional love both in the way he conveyed respect and affirmation, and in the way he challenged me to surrender more fully to God in Jesus Christ. He taught me how to connect all my joys and sorrows to Christ and to God's Holy Word in the Scriptures. He also exposed me to Byzantine prayers, insights and liturgies. I still carry with me his insights, his manner, his prayerfulness, and I seek to emulate these with those I encounter in my ministry.

Jesus calls us to a new way of being in the world. What this means for the spiritual journey of marginal persons such as women is that God's redeeming action is taking place right now as they seek their own liberation and that of others. Far from supporting the oppression of women, Jesus' vision calls forth elimination of structures of domination and submission. All who call themselves his disciples share this prophetic mission. The stories of women in the New Testament portray the liberating power of Jesus' presence and message.[38]— *Kathleen Fischer*

Lenora – The youth minister in my home parish became a real inspiration and a source of encouragement to me. He involved us young people in a way that was fun and considerate of our youthful interests and preferences. He helped us to read the Bible with some understanding and relevance to our lives. Later on in university, I connected with campus ministry and found similar support there.

To examine frequently our thoughts, words, and actions in the different situations in which we may find ourselves, and to do so in the light that radiates from our Lord, whom we are to imitate – in the light of the Holy Spirit who guided him always – to weigh everything in relation to the divine glory, will show us clearly whether we are under the influence of the Holy Spirit or our own. This little recommendation counseling a careful watch of our reactions is not intended to make us concentrate on our faults. Rather can it be a means of keeping the presence of God.[39]— *Mother Aloysius Rogers, OCD*

Elaine – My mom continues to be my role model. She is a strong woman who knows how to carry her vocation as mother in harmony with her liberating views on women, all based on her deep faith in Jesus.

Audrey – One of the people who served as a model for my ministry is a Lutheran woman pastor of an inner-city worshipping community. She models for me what it is like for a woman to be in a role of liturgical presider. She is also a shining example of faith in action with a real commitment to social justice and being in relationship with those who are most broken and rejected in our society.

Francine – I can't think of one particular person, but what comes to mind are the number of pioneer women who settled in new territory, who took a risk and who lived from a deep vision of what could be. They were founders of religious communities, missionaries, teachers moving across the prairies; they had a sense of moving into the unknown with deep faith and courage.

... the sweetness of the Holy Spirit is boundless and swift to encompass all creatures in grace, and no corruption can take away the fullness of its just integrity. Its path is a torrent, and streams of sanctity flow from it in its bright power, with never a stain of dirt in them; for the Holy Spirit itself is a burning and shining serenity, which cannot be nullified, and which enkindles ardent virtue so as to put all darkness to flight.[40]— *Hildegard of Bingen*

Happy, indeed, is the one to whom it is given to share this sacred banquet, to cling with all her heart to God whose beauty all the heavenly hosts admire unceasingly, whose love inflames our love, whose contemplation is our refreshment, whose graciousness is our joy, whose gentleness fills us to overflowing, whose remembrance brings a gentle light, whose fragrance will revive the dead, whose glorious vision will be the happiness of all the citizens of the heavenly Jerusalem.[41]— *Clare of Assisi*

Epilogue

This has been an amazing journey. The women, the conversations, the phone calls and e-mails, the laughter and the tears, the writing – each has woven its way into my personal story and into my heart. The weaving features strong and colourful threads, creating a stunningly new tapestry of faithfulness and vision. Francine, Anne, Betty and Deanna weave generous offerings of ministry with exceptional resiliency. Elaine, Audrey, Lenora, Millie and Anne give extra strength through commitments of humility and integrity. Sharon, Marlene, Annette and Carla add abiding base colours of prayer, diligent study and discernment. Wylma, Darlene, Gladys and Susan bring bright red threads, reminding us of our obligation to the poor and vulnerable in our midst. Knowing myself part of this tapestry that stretches across history and denominations gives special strength, trust and courage. This belonging allows me to live out my ministry to the full, and then … let it all go on the wings of God's Holy Spirit, with the assurance that it finds a place in God's work of art.

I am reminded daily that we have the treasure of both our calling and our ministry in clay jars. Wylma expressed it well when she described finding an unusual and abiding strength in God while remaining "hidden" and often ignored within official church structures. Indeed, we are neither perfect nor alone. As Sharon and other women described, God bestows the call, often to our own greatest surprise. God bestows the gifts and equips for ministry those who are called. Even while our ministry may not fit into currently existing church categories, God is faithful and opens doors in creative and unexpected ways. This gives our calling an ongoing dynamic and fresh flavour.

This same dynamic also gives our witness enormous energy, an energy that is profoundly powerful as well as vulnerable. Maybe it is the kind of power Fr. Ron Rolheiser speaks about in one of his columns, a power called *exousia* – vulnerable power, akin to the vulnerable power of a baby to evoke love and affection.[42] We walk by faith, without guarantees, without much automatic affirmation or formal mandate. Lenora, as well as Darlene and Wylma, illustrated this by sharing the developments of their ministries under several bishops. Because an automatic place in ministry (as is the case for priests) is missing, Catholic women find themselves re-evaluating opportunities, direction and choices for ministry much more frequently than their ordained colleagues. The tenuous nature of ministry jobs forces this type of frequent revisiting of choices and options; this is both invigorating and challenging.

Nearly two years have passed between the original writing and the publication of this book. In these two intervening years, several women have reported a change in their employment; in some cases, the change has led to a return to the world of secular work. While many women continue to find fulfillment and joy in their ministry, others find themselves faced with closed doors or with a level of pain that cannot be sustained. Not long ago I received the following e-mail:

> I've been meaning to write and say hello but have been very busy. I gave the parish notice of resignation this week. I have found the atmosphere around here very strange and I don't feel that this is the right time for me to be in this position. The parishioners here have been wonderful but the lack of communication and the cultural differences have been more than I have the energy to tackle. I have learned a lot in the short time but I had to get out before I got too attached. I have a tendency to fall in love with people very quickly and I already feel guilty for leaving. I feel even greater appreciation for the laity and the level of respect that I was given in other dioceses. I was blessed to always work with Canadian-born priests who showed me great respect, friendship and value while appreciating my creativity and giving me complete control over my job and responsibilities.

> This position has been very odd right from the interview. I fear that this may be an even greater problem as some bishops move farther away from the involvement of the laity to the importation of priests from very different lands.

I feel a great deal of relief and will continue to discern my role in the Church. I guess parishes are like families: no one knows what goes on behind closed doors. I worked at parishes in various dioceses over the course of a decade and have never experienced the strange dynamic that exists here.

I myself have been involved in yet another period of discernment and scrutiny. A number of factors led to a decision to step back from active ministry and resume studies. Once again I needed to listen carefully to what life-giving direction my spirit needed, and which doors God's Spirit was opening both in my own heart and in the Church universal. Again I faced questions about vocation, about windows of opportunity, and about how to find faithful expressions of my calling. Nothing is fixed for Catholic women in ministry, nothing is guaranteed, and nothing in our employment is protected by ecclesiastical structures.

The stories and insights shared in this book are by definition incomplete. Much, much more needs to be said, to be reflected on, and to be critically analyzed. The voices of priests and married laymen in ministry need to be added to the women's voices in this book. Here in western Canada, some dioceses – my own included – are animated by a vision for ministry and ecclesial leadership that includes lay people in most creative and appropriate ways. At the level of the Western Conference of Catholic Bishops, however, little corporate guidance and theological reflection has been provided regarding the ordering of lay ecclesial ministry. This corporate episcopal silence stands in contrast to the Quebec Catholic bishops, who have published an impressive collection of reflections and guidelines on lay ecclesial ministry in French for the past 35 years. Without negating the great strides made in individual dioceses, scant episcopal guidance and reflection can play havoc with job security, appropriate mandate and blessing, role definition and justice issues for both male and female lay people in ministry.

The witness in this book is splashed with tears – tears of both joy and sorrow. The vulnerability and boldness that characterize the women's contributions have been left largely intact. There are some risks in adopting this approach. One is that the reader will dwell on the negatives and forget about the deep joy and satisfaction that many women report in their day-to-day dealings with people in their ministerial roles. It is important to keep in mind that human beings focus on what's wrong; God focuses on what's right, making even pain bear fruit.

The other risk is one that Rev. Donald Cozzens speaks about in his book *Sacred Silence*:

> Personal experience as well as our collective memory make it clear that to speak the truth as one sees it, no matter that it is spoken "in love," runs the risk of being perceived as disloyal. Certain practices, structures, customs, and beliefs, even if they are clearly open to historical development, are judged by the controlling polity as too dangerous to address. To nonetheless speak one's truth, even the simple call for discussion of neuralgic issues invites the charge of disloyalty. And when the verdict of disloyalty is passed, the subject under judgment experiences some degree of psychological and social isolation.[43]

Lest any reader risk concluding that insights and experiences of Catholic women in ministry lead to ecclesial disloyalty, Cozzens reminds us that it is precisely a deep love and loyalty "to the gospel and the institutional church that often prompts the breaking of an unholy silence, that brings a man or woman to speak respectfully and directly [...] about what matters to them most."[44] I think here also of the bold witness of Canadian Religious Conference, an association of Canadian religious orders, in March 2006 when they wrote their letter to the Canadian Conference of Catholic Bishops to help them prepare for their *ad limina* visit to Rome. The letter was prefaced as follows: "We would like to share our concerns, our questions, our sufferings, as well as those of our brothers and sisters. We do this in a spirit of faith and communion, as People of God, faithful to Jesus Christ and his Gospel."[45]

I can concur with these words. I have written this book with a similar deep love and affection for the Roman Catholic Church. It seems nigh impossible to abandon this Church in a spirit of indifference or defiance, as so many have done and continue to do. "Mother Church" is the womb that bore me, the nest in which both my faith and my calling were conceived, nurtured and grew in maturity and depth.

"Mother Church" gladly gives birth to our Catholic faith. What she does need to learn better, however, as any good mother knows, is the virtue of letting her children grow up and allowing them to sit as mature adults at the family table, where their voices matter in significant conversations and decisions.

Notes

1   Margaret Lavin, *Theology for Ministry* (Ottawa: Novalis, 2004).

2   Topsy is the name of a "ragamuffin" young slave girl of unknown origin, a character in Harriet Beecher Stowe's book *Uncle Tom's Cabin*, which was published in 1852. The phrase "growed like Topsy" (later, "grew like Topsy" – now somewhat archaic) passed into the English language, originally with the specific meaning of unplanned growth, later sometimes just meaning enormous growth. Source: http://en.wikipedia.org/wiki/Uncle_Tom's_Cabin

3   *Pacem in Terris*, no. 41. (All references to Vatican II documents are taken from *The Basic Sixteen Documents. Vatican Council II: Constitutions, Decrees, Declarations – A Complete Revised Translation in Inclusive Language*. Austin Flannery, OP, ed. Northport, NY: Costello Publishing Company, 1996.)

4   Christopher Marlowe, "The Passionate Shepherd to His Love."

5   Elizabeth Johnson, *Friends of God and Prophets* (Ottawa: Novalis, 1998), 219.

6   David DeLambo, *Lay Parish Ministers: A Study of Emerging Leadership* (Committee on the Laity of the U.S. Conference of Catholic Bishops, 2005).

7   See Francis Thompson's poem "The Hound of Heaven."

8   "Three icons were found in 1918 in a barn nearby the Church of the Dormition of Zvenigorod (decorated by Andrei Rublev and Daniel Chorny). All three were part of a Deisis. This icon of the Saviour is one of them, and it is certain that it has been painted by Andrei Rublev." (accessed 20/09/06) Source: http://www.iconsexplained.com/iec/00034.htm#background

9   Chapter I, par. 10, *Sacrosanctum Concilium*, Constitution on the Sacred Liturgy.

10   Chapter I, par. 14, *Sacrosanctum Concilium*, Constitution on the Sacred Liturgy.

11   http://www.essene.com/MaryMagdalene.htm (accessed 31/07/06).

12   Joseph Martos, *Doors to the Sacred: A Historical Introduction to the Sacraments in the Catholic Church* (Tarrytown, NY: Triumph Books, 1991).

13   In Alcoholics Anonymous, the Fourth Step involves writing an inventory of all one's sins, offences and hurts; the Fifth Step calls for sharing this list with another person.

14   http://www.catholicnews.com/data/stories/cns/0506784.htm (accessed 20/09/06).

15   Donald Cozzens, *The Changing Face of the Priesthood* (2000) and *Sacred Silence* (2002), both published by Liturgical Press, Collegeville, MN.

16   Richard Gaillardetz, "Marriage and Salvation, *Our Family Magazine*, January 2001, 3.

17   Donald Cozzens, *The Changing Face of the Priesthood* (2001), and *Sacred Silence* (2002).

18   Cozzens, *Sacred Silence*, 112.

19   Ron Rolheiser, *The Holy Longing: The Search for a Christian Spirituality* (New York: Doubleday, 1999).

20   Cozzens, *The Changing Face of the Priesthood* (2001) and *Sacred Silence* (2002).

21   Eugene Kennedy, *The Unhealed Wound: The Church and Human Sexuality* (New York: St. Martin's Press, 2001), 117.

22   *Lay Parish Ministers: A Study of Emerging Leadership*, http://www.usccb.org/laity/laymin/research.shtml (click on "Executive Summary"). Accessed 31/07/06.

23   Reginald Bibby, *Restless Churches: How Canada's Churches Can Contribute to the Emerging Religious Renaissance* (Ottawa: Novalis, 2004).

24   "In the First Principle and Foundation [the Introduction to the *Spiritual Exercises*], Ignatius spoke of a spirituality of detachment. Detachment is an awareness of priority and the proper usage of created things. This awareness can free us from anything that might destroy our relationship with God. Attachments in themselves are not problems; they become problematic

when they take the place of God in our lives. All things are gifts from God to help us toward living in union with God. They are not to replace God. Therefore, we should and ought to use whatever brings us closer to God, and get rid of whatever separates us from God. There often is a misunderstanding about this aspect of Ignatian spirituality: "the end justifies the means." No, we use created things as God meant them to be used in order to lead us in fulfillment of God's individual plan for us." http://www.donghanh.org/main/1td_ld_007_short_intro.htm. For more information on Ignatian spirituality, see http://www.bc.edu/bc_org/prs/stign/ignatian_spirit.html. Accessed 31/07/06.

[25]   Sheila Cassidy, *Audacity to Believe* (London: Darton, Longman and Todd, 1992).

[26]   *Catechism of the Catholic Church*, no. 1782.

[27]   Margaret Dorgan, *St. Teresa of Avila: A Guide for Travel Inward* (Kalamazoo, MI: Cistercian Publications, 1987), 351.

[28]   Mary Ward as quoted by Mary Malone, *Christian Women: A New Vision* (Dubuque, IA: Brown Roa, 1985), 99.

[29]   Blessed Mary MacKillop, unpublished manuscript, Sisters of St. Joseph, North Sydney, Australia, as quoted in *People's Companion to the Breviary*, Carmelites of Indianapolis, 1977.

[30]   Thérèse of Lisieux, *The Story of a Soul: The Autobiography of St. Thérèse of Lisieux*. Translation by John Clarke OCD, Discalced Carmelites. (Washington, DC: ICS Publications, 1976), 194.

[31]   Marjorie Hewitt Suchocki, *God, Christ, Church* (New York: Crossroads Publishing, 1989), 132.

[32]   Antoinette Doolittle, as quoted by Robley Edward Whitson, ed. in *The Shakers: Two Centuries of Spiritual Reflections* (Mahwah, NJ: Paulist Press, 1983), 351.

[33]   Edith Stein, *The Hidden Life* (Washington, DC: ICS Publications, 1992), 115.

[34]   Thérèse of Lisieux, *The Story of a Soul*, 194.

[35]   Margaret Quigley & Michael Garvey, eds. *The Dorothy Day Book* (Springfield, IL: Templegate Publishers, 1982), 59.

[36]   Catherine of Siena, *The Dialogue* (Mahwah, NJ: Paulist Press, 1980), 25.

[37]   Dorothy A. Vidulich, *Peace Pays a Price: A Study of Margaret Anna Cusack* (Sisters of St. Joseph of Peace, 1990), 15, 70.

[38]   Kathleen Fischer, *Women at the Well: Feminist Perspectives and Spiritual Direction* (Mahwah, NJ: Paulist Press, 1988), 83.

[39]   Mother Aloysius Rogers, OCD, *Fragrance from Alabaster* (New Hampshire: Carmelite Monastery, 1961), 24.

[40]   Hildegard of Bingen, *Scivias* (Mahwah, NJ: Paulist Press, 1990), 37.

[41]   Clare of Assisi, *Francis and Clare: The Complete Works* (Mahwah, NJ: Paulist Press, 1982), 204.

[42]   Ron Rolheiser, "The Cross as Revealing the Non-violence of Christ," February 10, 2002, www.ronrolheiser.com.

[43]   Donald Cozzens, *Sacred Silence*, 12–13.

[44]   Ibid., 14.

[45]   http://www.crc-canada.org/bd/fichierNouveaute/284_2.pdf (accessed 20/09/06).

Web Resources for Laypeople in Ecclesial Ministry

In Canada

Assemblée des évêques catholiques du Québec
www.eveques.qc.ca

Canadian Conference of Catholic Bishops
www.cccb.ca

Réseau Ministeria Network Canada
www.ministeria.org

> The Réseau Ministeria Network is a Canadian forum aimed at supporting all lay persons working in ecclesial ministry and providing opportunities for growth by the sharing of experiences, stories, wisdom and faith. It is an ecclesial network, open to all (lay persons, permanent deacons, priests and bishops) but centred on lay ecclesial ministers, their ministries, their life, their vocation and their spirituality.
>
> The network is not an association, or a movement, or a group of action claiming. It is an open, supple space offering an opportunity to all interested persons to pray and reflect on the ministries exercised by lay persons for the mission of the Church. No participation fee or diocesan subscription is required.

In the United States

National Association for Lay Ministry
www.nalm.org

Center for Applied Research in the Apostolate
www.georgetown.edu/research/CARA

Conference for Pastoral Planning and Council Development (CPPCD)
www.cppcd.org

National Association of Church Personnel Administrators (NACPA)
www.nacpa.org

National Association of Pastoral Musicians
www.npm.org

National Conference for Catechetical Leadership (NCCL)
www.nccl.org

National Catholic Young Adult Ministry Association (NCYAMA)
www.ncyama.org

National Federation for Catholic Youth Ministry
www.nfcym.org

National Pastoral Life Centre
www.nplc.org

United States Conference of Catholic Bishops Secretariat for Family, Laity, Women and Youth
www.usccb.org/laity

Catherine of Siena Institute
www.siena.org

Marie-Louise Ternier-Gommers

Finding the Treasure Within

A Woman's Journey into Preaching

Foreword by Ron Rolheiser, OMI

Winner, First Time Author of a Book award,
Catholic Press Association, 2003!

What do you do when you discover your voice but cannot find a way to express it? Marie-Louise Ternier-Gommers, a Roman Catholic laywoman, faced this challenge. Growing up in the Netherlands and inspired by the spirituality of the Taizé community in France and Jean Vanier's L'Arche community, she lived her faith fully. When she moved to Canada to marry a Saskatchewan farmer, the prairie life invited her into a new way of experiencing God. Making their living off the land, she and her family stayed involved in numerous aspects of church and community life. Once her three children were in school, she made time to pursue theological studies in a Lutheran seminary, where she gradually discovered her gift for preaching.

Finding the Treasure Within is about the joy and pain of discovery written by a passionate defender of both her church and her place within the community of God's people.

> "This is a good story, a true story, a hope-filled story. It is a story that needs to be told because it models how any of us, faced with a situation that does not seem fair, can find the way that leads through the narrow gate, the generative gate that opens the doorway to new life." —*from the Foreword, by Ronald Rolheiser*

Available from Novalis

NOVALIS

1-800-387-7164

www.novalis.ca

More and more people today are involved in ministry in some way: as lay pastoral assistants, chaplains, pastors, youth group leaders and more. But what is ministry? How do we do ministry, and why? In *Theology for Ministry*, Margaret Lavin leads readers through the underlying theological themes of this form of service – who we believe our God is, and who we are in relationship to God – in order to show how they inform what we do in ministry. Lavin's faith-filled approach draws out the pastoral implications of these themes and reminds us that each of us is called to minister in some way to the larger community. This resource will help those involved in ministry to find the theological roots they need in order to support and enrich their work with those around them as they grow in faith together.

"An invitation to open the windows again. A reminder of what we might lose."—*Lucinda Vardey, editor of* God in All Worlds & The Flowering of the Soul

"In simple contemporary language Margaret Lavin explains why and how all baptized Christian believers are equipped and empowered to minister to their neighbour. With suitable depth and contagious passion she draws on the Scriptures of the Old and the New Testament, on the doctrines of the Trinity and the Incarnation, and on the sacramental and liturgical tradition to show that, whether they are ordained or not, ministry can and should become an integral part of their life." —*Fr. George H. Tavard, Assumption Center, Boston*